AF413788

six feet short of the moon

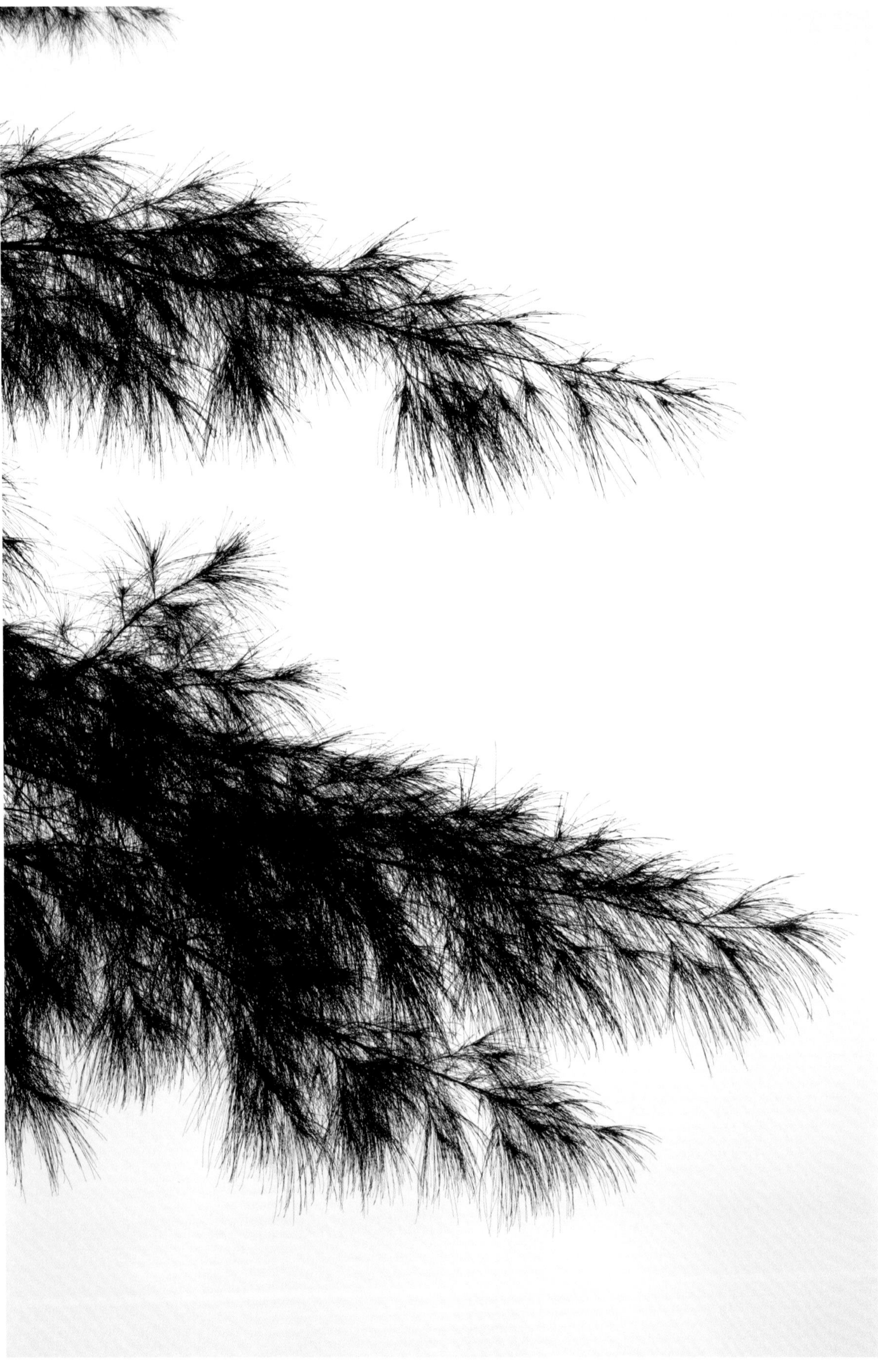

six feet short of the moon

poems by Matthew Wong

The Matthew Wong Foundation 2025

Contents

Introduction

John Yau

Shortly after I joined Facebook in 2012, mostly to post links to reviews I had started writing for Hyperallergic, Matthew Wong sent me a message. He told me that he lived in Hong Kong and that he had been unable to find one of my books, In The Realm of Appearances: The Art of Andy Warhol *(Ecco Press, 1993). After a few more exchanges, we agreed that I would send him a copy and, when he got it, he would send me a drawing, which he did. I did not know anything about Matthew but what he told me, which is that he had begun making drawings in ink. The drawing he sent me was done in pencil and dated 2012. I soon began following him on Facebook and deduced that he was using its network to teach himself about art. He posted questions, offered opinions, and seemed to be in touch with many people. He was encyclopedically voracious and often mentioned names of well-known and unknown artists in the same post. I only learned later that he was interested in poetry when he wrote me a note thanking me for my review of* A Dark Dreambox of Another Kind: The Poems of Alfred Starr Hamilton *(Song Cave, 2013), with a foreword coauthored by Ben Estes and Alan Felsenthal. This is how Estes and Felsenthal describe Hamilton:*

> *Terms such as* outsider, untrained, *and* peripheral *have all been applied to the poetry of Alfred Starr Hamilton. In introducing his work to a new generation of readers, we hesitate to apply these labels exclusively, for fear that their connotations may hinder readers from perceiving his poems as fully and consciously constructed—the real thing.*

In an autobiographical note, Hamilton wrote, "Poetry is the story of the search for freedom."

All of this came back to me as I read Wong's poems, written between 2009 and 2016. They are consciously constructed, as his early poems written in rhyme attest to. More important, they are the real thing, a record of a young artist-poet in search for freedom, which in Wong's case meant writing a poem that was unmistakably his. And yet, even in his first poems, the reader comes across lines that stand out: "Truth is, / When it's that quiet / The silence sounds more like a machine gun pouring its heart out to the world." It is too easy and dismissive to say "surrealism," as this line resists summation and analysis.

Memories, dread, and feelings of being cut off from other human beings mark Wong's poems, but he never becomes solipsistic. Art was his way of gaining agency. There is an unadorned plainness to his poems—a vulnerable directness that he was able to channel into dramatic monologues, autobiographical recollections, and liminal states. In titling two of his monologues, "The Pornographer" and "The Killer's Soliloquy," Wong picks extreme outsiders to become the vehicle through which he could reflect upon his own feelings of imploding loneliness. The opening lines of "The Killer's Soliloquy" are "Give me your daughter's irises, so I can dip them / In the kitchen's blood as a requiem for my remorse." The tension between Wong's inner and outer world is always acute. In the prose poem "The Passenger," he writes, "I shrink in my seat and fill my thoughts with foreign music."

Reading Wong's poems, I get a sense of what it was like to live in his body and mind, and see through his eyes. I reviewed Wong's debut exhibition in New York in 2018, which he titled The Realm of Appearances; *authored an essay for a catalog of his ink drawings,* Footprints in the Wind, Ink Drawings 2013–2017 *(Cheim & Read, 2021); and contributed to* Matthew Wong - Vincent van Gogh: Painting as a Last Resort *(Thames & Hudson, 2024). Whether painting, drawing, or writing poems, the subject of Wong's work was loneliness and his feeling of being forever outside, looking in. No matter how expansive a landscape he depicts in paint or evokes in words, his claustrophobic feelings of being stuck inside himself come through without devolving into a plea for pity or even compassion. In "Jealousy," he writes, "I am deep in the library, alone / In the way one is, or can be / Alone on a strange planet."*

In his art, Wong was able to communicate his deepest feelings, however dark and tormented they might be, without becoming cloying. That directness is why we stop and look or, in the case of his poems, pick up this book and read. Consider the world he conjured up in the prose poem "Vacuum":

> *In the northernmost point of China, where the nation is bordered by Russia and the moon, there is an apartment building of unspeakable architecture that is being guarded solely by a gaunt man who has forgotten his age. The man wears a pale blue security uniform that hangs off his body the way water falls from a bucket. There are no calendars here, and each unit contains neither door nor window. The inhabitants, sealed into their rooms by a facade of cement and ivory, pass the time by writing*

poetry on the walls with their fingertips, without sorrow, without hope, the words coming from a language that does not exist.

Overwhelmed at times with feelings of sorrow and hopelessness, as he must have been, Wong accomplished the miraculous. He made a haunting, broken world of harsh and tender beauty appear. In the painting, that world is landscapes. In the poems, it is cities and houses. In the last lines of his poem "They're Playing Our Song Again," he writes, "What are the chances / Of finding the rest of your life / Outside a poetry reading, anyway?" Wong understood the comfort that only a poem can give, no matter how brief the respite might be. That is why this book is urgent and necessary. For all the pain and solitude we encounter in these pages, there is also comfort and understanding.

The Land of Nod:
The Uncanny Spaces of Matthew Wong's Poems

John Wall Barger

My first conversation with Matthew Wong was in a cafe in Hong Kong, October 2012. I'd read at an open mic and he began chatting to me without being introduced. He liked a poem I'd read, and we immediately found ourselves— spurred by my (unremarkable) poem, to some extent—talking about the animal sexuality of Francis Bacon and violent surreality of David Lynch. I liked how Matthew skipped the small talk and jumped into the conversational deep end. We went out for Mexican food around the corner. I learned that he had a girlfriend (his last), was writing pieces for an online magazine as an art critic, and had just begun experimenting with ink drawings, inspired by a visit to the Venice Art Biennale the year before. We became Facebook friends and a few days later I received a message: "Hi John, Just out of curiosity—how hard is it to get one's poetry into The Nation *and* The New Republic? *Matt." So I had an inkling right away of how ambitious he was!*

We were friends for seven years. He was 28, I was 43. When not face to face, our correspondence (500 pages) was on Facebook Messenger. When I lived in Hong Kong (January 2012 to June 2014), we met frequently at poetry gatherings and at my village house in Tai Po, a bus ride away from where he lived in Mong Kok. In those years he began focusing all his attention on painting and writing poems. He traveled back and forth with his mother Monita to an art studio in Zhongshan, Canton province, China. We sat on a bench in front of my house and

talked for hours. Matthew was extremely smart. He seemed to have read everything, and knew the names of many artists and poets I'd never heard of. I loved talking to him. He chainsmoked cigarettes and I puffed on a cigar. He sipped on a bottle of iced tea, and I drank coffee. I read him a printed out stack of my poems, and he read me his off his phone. I visited his house just once: a tiny apartment with paintings all over the floor and on the kitchen table. He showed me the paintings, we talked for an hour, and I left.

To me, Matthew was almost always kind. He liked my poems and spoke to me with respect. From all our conversations and trading of work, I think we had a distinct effect on each other. One day he wrote me, "Hey John, I just finished a poem that's on my wall, stepped back to read it and realized I was writing in your voice. Spooky. Wrote it real quick and spent last hour editing. Didn't start out like your voice but kinda got there thru the drafts, weird. . ."

He spoke honestly, bluntly—and this made communication uncomfortable sometimes. If he hated a poem of mine, no matter how excitedly I presented it, he'd say so. He was very tall, but quiet: hovering at the edge of the group. You forgot he was there, but then he would cut in a conversation with a snippet of hip hop, or a joke that didn't always make sense. At open mics, he'd sometimes read a poem and leave without a word. Socially, Matthew never found a way to express vulnerability. He masked his sadness with a scowl. As a kid he'd been bullied, which might have left him mistrustful. Many were put off by his awkwardness and excluded him from parties and gatherings. He noticed, of course, and took it hard. He once came to blows with an (arrogant) member of our circle at Joyce Is Not Here, the bar where the English-speaking poets gathered. And he had altercations with many others. A friend of ours, Nicolette Wong, told me he once asked her out of the blue if she thought he was a genius. Another night he wrote her, "Looking into your world is like looking into a black hole." She replied, "Your world is even darker than mine—nobody could see into it."

"I hate to be brash," he wrote me once, "but I think I may be a genius." Like me, he was an only child. He (like me) could be paranoid and self-centered. Matthew was open about having Tourette's, and later I learned he'd been diagnosed with autism. I found him increasingly difficult to talk to, as he continually changed the topic to himself and his painting. At a certain point, around 2016 or 2017 (when I'd left Hong Kong and lived in a village in Dharamsala, India), Matthew didn't seem willing or able to sustain a conversation outside of his own direct interests. So we drifted. I was aware that he was painting like mad, and that he wanted to become famous. I told people I had a friend who is trying to become famous through social media! Every time my partner Tiina saw his string of new paintings on Facebook, one of us would inevitably say, "Hell, look how good Matthew's getting!"

We lost contact altogether in 2017 when he moved to Edmonton and dropped off Facebook. I wrote friends asking about him but none had heard from him. I was dimly aware that he was becoming well known, but did not know the extent. He came back online in 2018, but we never really got back on track with our correspondence.

One of our last back and forths was about Cy Twombly's paintings, who he loved. I sent a picture from Fifty Days at Iliam, *on a visit to the Philadelphia Museum of Art. I told him I wanted to make poems as big and iconic as those paintings, and he agreed. But there was no excited back and forth.*

He died by suicide in Edmonton, October 2, 2019.

.

This book is a selection of my favorite Matthew Wong poems. Since many of these were hibernating in my Facebook inbox for years, I personally am very excited that they will see the light of day. For reasons that I'll try to explain, his poems have merit not just in accompaniment with his dazzling paintings, but also on their own. They deserve a place at the poetry table.

When I first met him, Matthew was posting poems every few days on Facebook Notes, all of which vanished when he deleted his account. I always liked his poems, but didn't think they were brilliant initially. The first ones I saw, like "Inspirado" and "Smoke," seemed overly indebted to Charles Simic: surreal but not yet transcendent. Like Matthew's paintings, his poems improved extremely fast.

His writing process, as he described it to me at one point, was to type a poem into his iPhone, until its size roughly fit the length and width of the screen. My sense was that he completed poems quickly, in one fell swoop, but sometimes he surely spent longer. In reference to two (lost) poems, "First Month" and "Janitorial Blues," he wrote me, "i was definitely paying more attention and working them out for a good hour or two before i considered them acceptable." After finishing a poem, he told me he'd send it immediately to a journal—usually high profile, like The New Yorker *or* Paris Review—*and also sent a copy to me. He once wrote, showing that he had a sense of humor about the notes he received, "i got a rejection today: 'I'm sorry to take so long with this poem, only to have to pass on it. It has some very strong moments, but some soft spots too. Please do try us again. though.'—[response] sounds like my sex life!"*

One day Matthew wrote out of nowhere: "just did a weird drawing that simultaneously references plant life but also crown of thorns and fall from grace..." It's fun to know people who are working hard on their craft! It's contagious. Our conversations, in person and online, moved fluidly from art to poetry to pop culture to personal anecdotes. Aside from being strongly inspired by Matthew's commitment to making art and his discipline, I learned a lot from our conversations. Concepts we both loved, like duende and the uncanny, seemed to evolve as we spoke, and integrated into our work. I loved Lorca's essay on duende and referred to parts often, like this: "'Viva Paris!' As if to say: We are not interested in aptitude or techniques or virtuosity here. We are interested in something else." When I sent Matthew the essay, he responded, "Finally read the Lorca. I can see the quality of this force in some of the best among the poems i've read from you, but I do not think I have arrived at this state with my poetry yet. I think it may have struck me one or two times in my paintings." The first poems Matthew sent me, like "Smoke," seemed to self-consciously reach for death, or duende: "Outside the nightclub. / I asked her, / 'Are your folks home?'/ She ran a finger / Across her neck, /'Dead.'" Later, I think Matthew's poems land on a powerful balance between humor and darkness—or something else.

Matthew, like many young writers, once loved Ginsberg and Kerouac, but finally concluded that "the beat state of mind is a perpetually ado-lescent thing." He wrote me, "yeah my first stint at Joyce's i was into the Beat thing... i think the absence was good for me to wait till i outgrew it and could think about things in a more grounded perspective. groundedness is good for writing, all art actually..." Matthew was extremely literate. He'd taken his B.A. at the University of Michigan, and read widely his whole life. He referred often to Raymond Carver, Bret Easton Ellis, David Foster Wallace. He was electrified by poets Michael Palmer, Rae Armantrout, Lorine Niedecker, Graham Foust, James Arthur, and "surrealists" like John Ashbery, James Tate, Mark Strand, and Simic. Of Palmer, Ashbery, and Tate he wrote, "i feel like those guys are impossibly distant from me achievement—wise but when i read their words i feel a shudder of familiarity as if it was something in me all along."

The extended focus Matthew gave his art was incredibly inspiring. That, I think, is how talent turns to genius. Matthew knew he wanted to make art, but wasn't positive what type. When I met him he quit photographs and began painting compulsively. He wrote poems consistently, then not at all for months. He sent me only about ten poems in the first year I knew him. But then, about October 2013, he wrote like a madman, almost a poem a day for six weeks. The lion's share of this book is from this period. That's when his poems took a jump forward and "thickened," in my opinion.

In October 2013, Matthew's dream-spaces shifted from self-consciously "weird" to deeply distinctive and haunting. He referred often to James Arthur's poem, "The Land of Nod" (from Charms Against Lightning, Copper Canyon, *2012—which Matthew and I passed back and forth and read from aloud), which I think helped him navigate and enter the "space" of his poems. Arthur's poem ends this way: "As a grown man, I've heard that Nod/never was a nation—of Cain's offspring, or anyone— / but a mistranslation of "wander," so Cain / could go wherever, and be in Nod. Far more / than in God, I believe in Cain, who destroyed / his own brother, and therefore in any city / could have his wish, and be alone." Art was, I think, Matthew's Land of Nod: a inner space where he could create allegorical worlds, exert a bit of power over his life, avoid the painful world around him, and "wander." But there is no forgiveness for Cain, or any of us, because we carry Nod, the place of punishment, inside ourselves.*

Charles Simic, master of uncanny menacing landscapes, had a big influence on Matthew's early poems. Compare Simic's "Gospel" ("Half-way to nowhere— / I thought I heard / Church bells ringing, / The blind man on the corner / Call out my name") with the end of Matthew's poem, "Far": "I looked up / Towards the Venetian sky, squinting / Past a pair of birds, and waited / For someone to call my name.

The uncanny—a concept Matthew mentioned constantly—refers (in Freud's sense of Unheimliche*) to something both familiar and alien. I think Matthew saw himself and his work this way: inside and outside of his environment, familiar and alien. Julia Kristeva's idea of abjection describes something that doesn't fit into the conventional order, and is cast out. The abject being, trying to fit in, is traumatized. But Matthew's sense of the uncanny, as Sun Man Ho said, might more accurately be described as "Wongian." The concept, for Matthew, had evolved beyond language into a certain something else. I once posted a black and white picture of my grandmother from the 1940's on Facebook: she was smiling, sweetly, with dimples, in a fur coat, snow and trees behind her. Matthew commented that it was the most uncanny image he'd ever seen, which left me scratching my head.*

Matthew's poems were suddenly murderously good. At some point—possibly through painting—something in him clicked: he'd negotiated the uncanny, surreal, funny, sad,

allegorical "space" of his poems. What do you say when your "weird" friend sends you a poem like this on Facebook Messenger?

*Whoever said that no man
Is an island is a fool, for are you not
At this moment wet and stranded
Among my outer wreckage,
Praying for the sting of salt to go away?
("The Island")*

His poem "True Romance" is titled, as Matthew liked to do, after a pop culture touchpoint (cf. "History of Violence," "Yesterday"), which immediately conveys a familiar context. But, as you can tell from the first lines, "True Romance" is not Tarantino: "The rainbow had been taunting us / With its beauty for the past half-hour." The speaker admires the rainbow— "you with your delicate / Curves we can't touch or drink from / Or make love to"—but eventually decides, "Honestly, / I'd rather be here, not up there. . ." It's erotic, though the object of affection remains veiled. The turn in the poem, from admiration of the rainbow to something else, arrives with the line, "The dirt / I am sitting on is wet with self-pity. / Brown, don't feel so bad." This "wet with self-pity" steps beyond the sad-in-the-rain trope, I think, into sublime territory. Almost synesthetic. Deliciously close to pathetic fallacy (the poetic taboo of attributing human feelings to inanimate objects), and containing an inimitable "Wongian" logic. In his later poems, like "Ned," he treads effortlessly into this zen koan-like, mind-bending space: "And his hat seemed to be providing / The sound of wayward flight." "Vincent," which might have been the last poem Matthew wrote, ends this way: "The moon / Is the color of remembering."

Like his paintings, Matthew's poems seemed to have been drawn from imagination, without "realistic" or literal observations. "Purpose" begins in a space of surreal symbols and figurative gestures:

"To kiss a doorbell. To daydream naked / Into the yellow pages. To whisper / Sweet nothings over a graveyard / Full of strangers." These are our purposes in the most liminal sense. But then the poem shifts into more recognizable landscape: "To hold indeterminacy / Hostage, permanently. To pick a number / From one to a million, and to build / A life around that number. / To write a blank cheque / Addressed to the rain." Suddenly we're in psychological terrain. These lines might describe Matthew's history, struggling at a practical job (trainee at Pricewaterhouse for six months), at school (bored senseless taking an M.F.A. in photography at CityU in Hong Kong)—then, finally, being an artist, where indeterminacy (and determination and focus) is key. In other words, "to build / A life" in the art world, or find recognition for your talent, would be as unlikely as writing "a blank cheque / Addressed to the rain."

Some of Matthew's poems tell the story of an awkward loner whose attempts to fit in result in struggle and suffering. In "Yesterday"—although the speaker distances himself by using past tense, muted emotions, and surreal images—the resemblance to the poet himself is unmistakable: "I made strange faces, sang songs / I heard my mother sing during / The childhood I never had…" Matthew had Tourette's, which made his face sometimes twist uncontrollably. And he would burst into conversations, which he didn't know how to enter organically, with song lyrics: is… and if / I got really excited, I screamed / A bottomless scream that was without / Angst or malice."

The end of "Yesterday" contains a wonderful softness, balancing all that pain, which I associate with Matthew's most powerful work: "I could not remember / Whether it was dark or light the moment / I finally went to sleep, but here we are, / And hello, sunshine." No matter how dark or bizarre his poems get, a sweetness—almost corniness—often comes with it, as if from the

same wellspring. Sometimes he sets his poems in "romantic" places ("Sunny capri," Venice, Varadero ["Viva Paris!"]) in an attempt to balance, I think, the cynical undertones. These images can border on cliché; but—as with his use of pathetic fallacy and synesthesia—Matthew somehow makes it work.

His paintings, I think, contain this same balance between soft and hard. Sweet images, very close to tropes—sunsets, lone figures, candles burning out, empty paths, footsteps in snow—are placed in savage and catastrophic landscapes. In "End of the Day," a small figure is dressed in white on the shore of a lake beside a great blue cosmic forest. "Night Crossing" portrays a small figure in a canoe, under a monstrous god-like tree, amid a billion stars. The collective story: we are all miniscule figures at the edge of a great wilderness, shored between worlds, cold, separate.

It's important to mention, I think, that this "corniness" was not something Matthew could express in life. He reserved it for his art. He— the only child, whose sole consistent influence throughout his life, his constant caregiver, was his mother Monita—never found a way, as far as I know, to be that soft with the people around him. He, himself, was on the shore between worlds. He pushed everyone away, unfriending us all on social media, over and over, and finally moving to Edmonton where he knew nobody but his mother.

Matthew once explained his philosophy to me, regarding the necessary balance between soft and hard in art, in reference to Matisse:

> *good for you that you have the courage to come out with cruel poems. i think violence is a necessary character for a great artist… Matisse was violent behind that deceptive pleasantness… i mean the paintings not the man… more needed than ever now perhaps… there are instances of psychological violence in Matisse's paintings at least to my*

*eye. . . a kind of dispassionate bluntness with
which he tacks on the paint to render figures, a
lot of psychological unease in fact, the beauty
of the color harmonies and what not are a
red herring. . .*

*Matthew's last poem, "Vincent," certainly
combines "deceptive pleasantness" with
"psychological violence." In his earlier—and less
mature, I think—poem, "The Passenger," the speaker
sees his reflection in a window: "I pretend to be
looking past him, at my reflection in the window,
but this only makes me recognize the ridiculousness
of my own appearance." By the time he wrote
"Vincent," Matthew had moved past literal mirrors
and ego and into an entirely figurative, visionary
space: "I study / My reflection in a tree, which
sings / Back to me in a playful tone / The outline of
a skull." The poem speaks to Van Gogh's trammeled
frustration, his "sorrow and longing," as well as that
of the poet. In Matthew's work, ideas like duende
and uncanny had evolved into an ineffable and
potent "Wongian" aesthetic.*

*It goes without saying that Matthew did finally
become a genius, I think, or perhaps had been one
all along. It's awful to consider that when Matthew
finally received the recognition he'd longed for, it
was not enough. It's awful that this friend of mine,
who I spoke to so often about death, whose poems
and paintings (with all their sadness and skulls
and duende) I encouraged, died by suicide. Was I
encouraging the man, or the desperation? Is art, as
I've always assumed, actually a cathartic, effective
way to release our psychic distress? It's awful to read
through my seven-year conversation with Matthew,
and to notice how I did not respond with enough
enthusiasm for him and his talent. I wish I'd told
him how much I admired him, and how much he'd
influenced me. He might have just laughed and told
me I was being corny.*

2009

Confetti

Remember the summer of '69?
How that football field stretched to forever
We'd lie down on the grass
Stare at the ceiling of the sky
Then go hand in hand
To inspect the reflection of us
In the transparent mirror of the jukebox.

A part of me still lives there
On the ragged front porch
Sitting, swinging idly while staring down the street
Waiting for you to materialize
Around the corner bend.

Since that watershed summer
The decades have trickled down on me
Falling like confetti into the past.

It's been 40 years since the summer of '69
Whenever I pause, quite often
To think of the football field
The jukebox
The front porch
The anticipation, every time like the first
I smile
Because it just goes to show
That through all this time
Some things change
While others never do.

Thoughts on the Number One

What would it look like,
If you tried to paint solitude?
If someone told me to image that,
I'd probably think of a Bel-Air house
Framed by white glass
On the inside,
A seductive shade of blue
That morphs subtly
According to changes in mood
That can be measured in nanometers
When it's that quiet
Everything gets counted.

Then I would imagine
Sitting on the ivory sofa
With an anachronistic handheld receiver
Where an indescribable woman speaks
She is not necessarily ineffably beautiful,
What I meant was
Her voice, when filtered through the waves
Sounds so that
You couldn't really tell what she looked like
As a matter of fact
You can't even picture that woman existing
As anything but that voice talking
In that exact moment, no before or after.
She would ask,
Are you lonely?
And you would reply,

As if out of movie dialogue,
I'm alone, I am not lonely.

Truth is,
When it's that quiet
The silence sounds more like a machine gun pouring its heart out to the world.

Tunnel Light

She was a girl of uptown disposition
Strutting around with sundown affectations
One night she went looking for some relaxation
Got caught in the cross fire
Of her one woman confrontation
Slumped by a graffiti wall, the writing says it all
Down on luck, out of love and flat line broke
Guess you could only hope to fall in sleep
On seas of wine driven by a wayward boat
Lids feeling slight, almost going out of sight
Saw a shadow traced in the distant edge
Of the pale, misty eyed worn-out moonlight
Summer must be in the air
When you faintly feel a warm embrace
A final blur
The horizon looked like that bedtime door
Where she once caught a glimpse of her father's face

Low

Some nights you go out cause you can't bear the view
If you're in luck, you might strike
The type who'd toss a couple chips of conversation
Out of regret or sympathy
Down here everybody's lost a few
I might be nobody but
There come times when even nobody needs a fool

Things crawling up my spine
That I can't explain
Could be the gamble of part-time gain
Or an angel's face reminds of roads that lead to pain
You think you need to hold on tight
With those sorry eyes stuck around in vain
Knowing damn well it's best to refrain

Your friends say they don't know me
Maybe
I'm not so sure that I do.

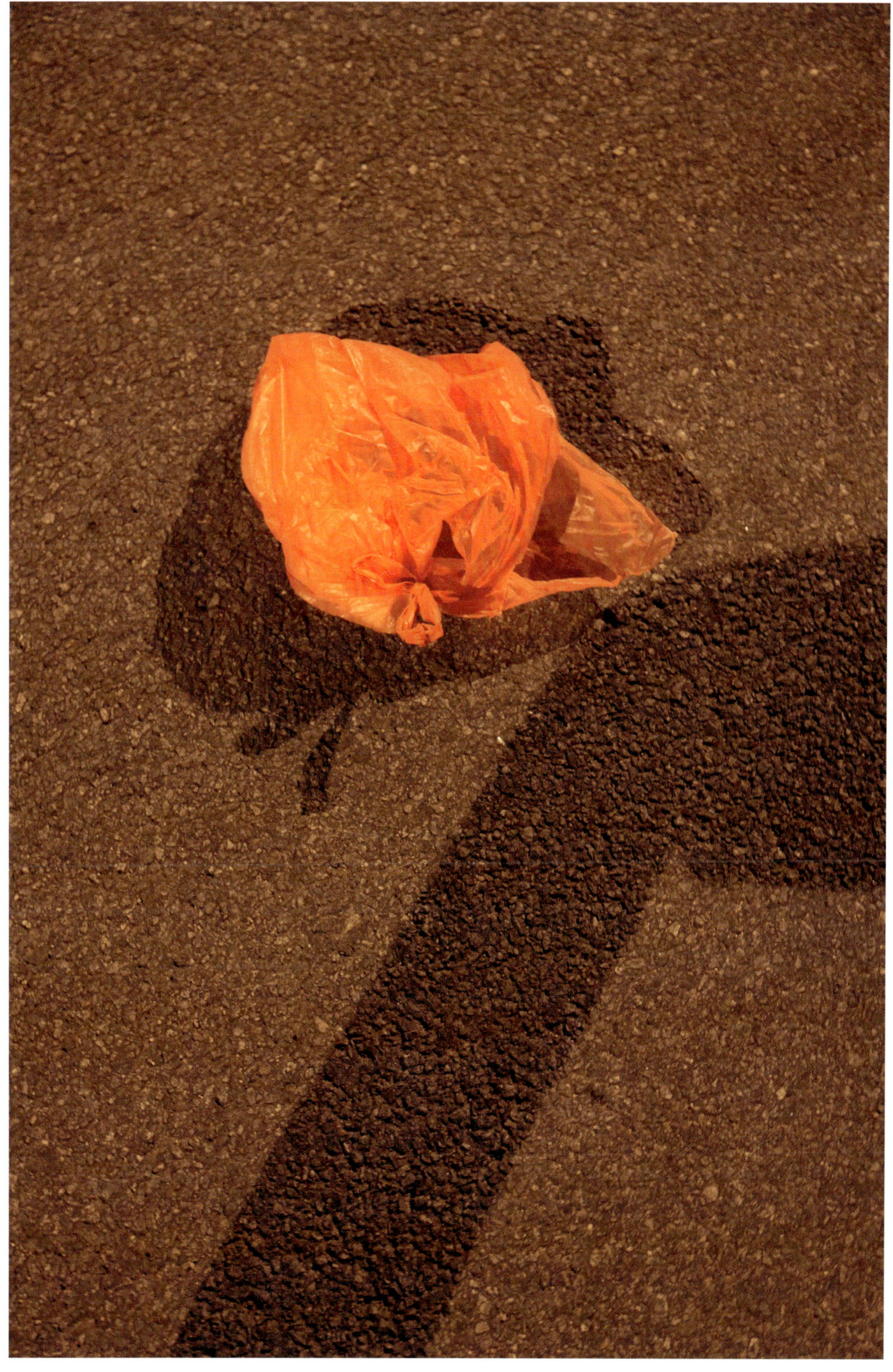

In the Middle

Dial those lights low now
Sit in the pillow soft silence
Watch those dancing shadows
Intertwine up by a lit window
If the summer breeze gets a bit slow
If these walls catch too much heat
I'll just take my thoughts through the door
Then carry them down and out to the street

Wandering my eyes on blank objects
Got a bound hand in each pocket
Fingers aimlessly strumming away
At loosely strung balls of denim thread
Down to my last two cigarettes
Figure I'll save them for another block
Still got to walk quite a while and a way
Before I find myself home on which to lay.

The lamp post bends and blinks
Seems like everything's had a drink
But I don't blame 'em, what else can you do
When all you got in your arms is an empty view
I could head back to bed and turn on the news
I could sit my ear by a radio playing the blues
So goes life in the middle of nowhere, nothing left or right
In other words, so goes life, in the middle of the night

Money

It so often occurs
Like a Peruvian handshake,
Or the three-way tango

Between ginger and a fox
And the id. We want to know
What gives meaning itself,

But always come up short,
Knowing we'd be better off in
the long run not knowing.

A Man in Full

As the bartender shouted 'Last Call!'
I was the only one there, if anybody was left at all
Thoughts I began to recall, of the road less taken
That got me where I was, and drove the stake in
The best compliment I ever got was 'fool!' she was far too kind
Only fools see holy water in a $5 bottle of wine
A source of daily baptism, embodying the essence of divine
In second place were virgins, in them, Jesus Christ, I could find
At 64, I still looked at high school girls with an aim
The older I got, the more they stayed the same
Sweet sixteens and forever seventeen is how my girls remained
From this I gained, all the pleasure, none of pain
I'd drive the paths they walked, no a fuck I did not give
Yet sometimes, give, give, give, give, give was all I did
Ah what it means to live, wrinkled and supple chunks of flesh
I never bought milk by the carton; I drank it from the breast
I might be old, bald, fat with a nasty crooked stare
But I was still vain and insecure, mirrors I couldn't bear
Women are often right. Too fucking smart for their own good
Maybe that's why they keep talking, instead of doing what they should
I see no problem with being just friends, mutual exchange of deeds
To me, a friend who at beck and call could bend, was a friend indeed
When I got bored, I'd throw 'em out like candy wrappers
If the lollipop's done and I chuck the paper, what really fuckin' matters?
I'd swagger, barge, brawl, slur, fuck and purr and purge
They were right; at 50 I got the body and face deserved

What purpose does a youthful handsome serve? Kids lack guts and glory
The useless, boring, banal backstory to the actual story
Life begins when you take your hands off the wheel
And place them on the hair and neck of the one who kneels
No, learn, I never did, wanted to or planned
I got old and delayed growing up, *I* was Peter Pan
Now everywhere I stand, I get fingers and jeers 'you dirty old man!'
Well, those suckers got one thing right —
I am nothing, absolutely nothing in this world, if not a man.

Little Ben and the Carousel

My memory purged the past, and just around the bend
I recalled a friend of mine, let's call him Little Ben
Small in stature, but a giant in heart and soul
As a boy he was so, so shy, so warm yet so cold
But when he stepped on stage, nobody else could glow
With such electricity, the stage was his, his life a show
He made the alphabet an immortal homage to puppy love
Girls clawed for his hands and heart, it came to push and shove
Those fragile fragile hands, they grew and he began to wear a glove
The mask hid and protected a heart shattered by years of ache
His past left in the dust, yet Little Ben's face was no mistake
And those gliding glimmering shoes, black as night and white as doves!
Time was hard, the road was tough, yet he didn't stop, even at enough
I'll never forget the night you took us all to walk the moon
Maybe it was outer space; time stopped, and we came back down far too soon
But on and on and on he rocked, making the disco ball his shining sun
A voice that never grew up, even as the clock would forever run
Perhaps a crack began to show, sadly the sun of human nature
Fame and fortune fleeting just as the wind flies by on a sheet of paper
The only constant in Little Ben's world were fairy tales
Cotton candy, carousels, pony rides and angels with ponytails
Soon the pressure made him frail, Little Ben had much to give
Too much, and he turned bad, the costume darker with each step he lived
The audience kept asking for more, Little Ben gladly obliged
Even as he doubted his state of mind, he remained happy outside
The years passed, Ben was little no more
But could not escape never never land, the world of grown-ups a bore
The father no longer scolded him, the brothers ceased the teasing
The damage was done though, those long-ago voices kept repeating
In his mind he is still the boy who deserved a beating

If he could not dance the night away, the crowd was his reason for being
Performance and reality soon mashed into a big old blur
The cheers and jeers followed suit, the wall of noise grew thick as fur
Further and further he retreated, from this world of disappointments and confusion
Into a happier illusion, animals and mannequins would be there to soothe him
The children still stayed the same, but Little Ben, alas did not remain
For his eternal fantasy, he paid the price and continued to let others gain
These days, I hear his health is not too well
That once glowing voice a shadowy whisper of a former shell
Who knows if it is show and tell, one last grasp at glory
What more did he need, to bring a happy ending to this story
Those old photos and songs of innocence, I treasure dearly
With a tear I conclude, for from the start, Little Ben was unhappy clearly
The tragedy, to everyone but him it could appear no clearer
Beautiful Little Ben, oh why can't you see the beauty in the man in the mirror

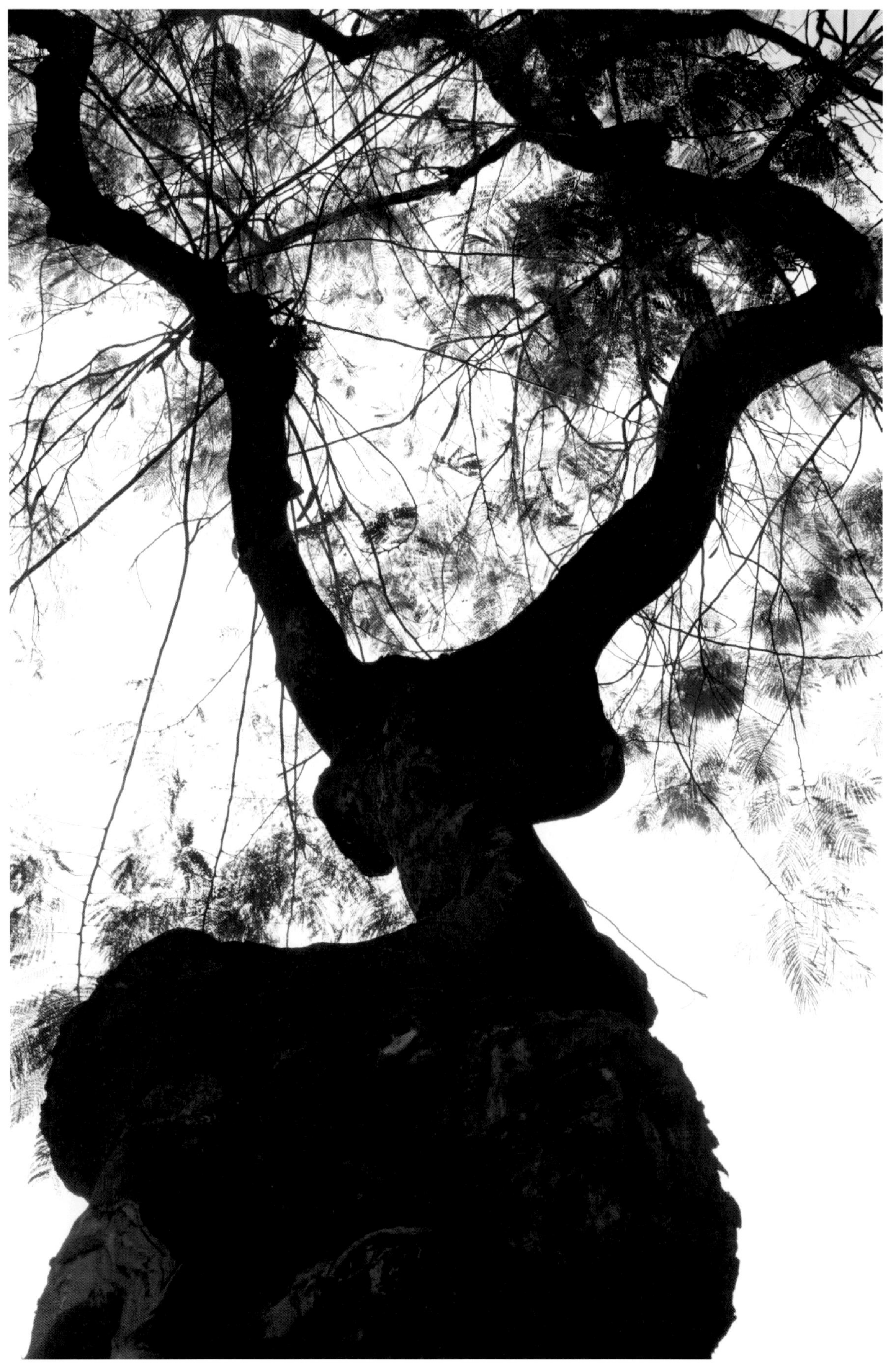

Elegy for a Gold Digger

Tell me, lately have you seen
A girl gone missing
Went by the name of Kitty Green
Might've passed through town
She would dip in and out
But never reached a shore beyond the scene
I first met her on the floor
Where she was crowned in glitter pour
A typical school-end teenage prom queen
Soon enough, time came and went
Flipping through the months like pages of a magazine
Men borrowed her, normally, older guys
Who forgot and liked to know
The feeling of, what it's like
To be stuck, well in between
The wishful walls of seventeen
Through record halls,
Behind movie screens,
Round revolving doors of bored hotels and art-filled galleries
There were brightly blurry days, star-lit lonely nights
She walked them in and out
But never grew the legs to flee the scene.

The Pornographer

You watch her move
Through the camera's eye
Projected on a glassy screen
She smiles at you
You smile back, sadly
She doesn't see.

How old are you
Is this your first time
You will always fail to forget those words
Forever, your first love.

Going through the motions
You assume a connection of emotions
After all, isn't that the only way to feel?
So she seems basked in the glow of enjoyment
You believe this can be real
Even though you remain faceless to her,
Forever your first love.

A tender schoolboy of sixteen
Watching in a hidden corner
As she passes by with a gang of guys
Then gives a fleeting glance in your direction
That unforgettable look
Containing so many meanings and intentions
Of which you will never know, sadly
Neither does she.

You don't care so much
For the close-up gaze
Into depravity and debauchery
The moment you wait for
Is her facial expression
Those eyes locked on yours,
Acknowledging that you are.

Forever your first love
Her whole head pursed in pleasure or pain
Is the picture framed in your memory
You watch her and smile,
But sadly, she never sees.

LA Confidential

As I
Stumbled upon the weary concrete
Tired of footsteps
Let alone my overbearing size 12 stamp
Some fishnet doe eyed brunette slurred my way
That she didn't have a place to sleep that night
Wanted to hitch a ride to heartbreak hotel
It was too good to be true
Because whenever it looks like true, it usually is good
And never true
We went to crash with a fifth of bourbon,
Jim's beam reminds her of childhood
Then we moved on to lemons and tequila,
Jose stung her like a salty promise
Held the whore in my arms, for she was me and I was her
We'd been down this road before,
The exit sign was right there, room 316
Glimmering in an entrance that only shined in VAC
The other four letters let to my imagination
Filthy, rotten, stinking, this carnal beast of burden
Let me know when it starts to hurt
And I'll drive it all the way home baby
Ain't no room in hell left for either of us anyway
No art, no suffering, I forgot about it 5 beers ago
No lingering poetic emotions or romance
Just two glasses clinking to a death that's been taking
Too damn long to show up at the door
Despite my repeat calls to room service
The fucking French toast was dangling somewhere like a hungover horizon
Her legs went open round and round,

Must've seen swankier revolving doors, this pretty woman
Except we were now forever filed into a little slice of motel life
On the California highway
By the detour that read "Heartbreak"
Population 6 billion
I refilled my tank,
Drove back onto the brisk LA morning
Turned to look at the number one more time
Clanking keys remembering me of another door closed
Suddenly
I felt so small
Like the rest of them.

Station

See that man sitting erect in the corner table
A lone parched pressed and clean figure
In a 4 AM den of sleaze, grease and badly done scrambled eggs
He is wearing horn rimmed glasses that read precision
A short sleeve button down shirt, presumably a scholar of Oxford
He quietly sips his coffee, then once finished arises
The gray flannel trousers reveal jarring pleats
Makes me wonder, what a man like this
Is doing at an ungodly moment of time like this
So I watch a single pleat
My imagination takes me running down the crease
Going for a loop through the cuffed hems
Up the inner lining
The destination is one that must lurk in any man
Let alone a man lurking these dim lit wastelands
Probably on the prowl
Desire directed by a cerebral conductor
A baton guides the unconscious primal urge
Spilling into a joint packed with inquisitive stares
The kind that wait for an anchor, and see if a ship wants to unload
Oh yes, I am no stranger to such docks
Figure this right here might be a kindred soul
Despite the splitting contrast between him and I
I guess what they say is true
We're not so different after all
Just when my half-baked musings grew more obtuse
Taking me into a conclusion of which I did not know the hypothesis
I am reminded of the common purpose
By the sound of a thick palm slamming onto the counter
A rumpled ten dollar bill

A brusque command—"keep the change"
Thigh high boots connected with threads of frayed cut-off denim
Amazonian guide to this jungle, escorting our mild-mannered friend out the door
Once more, I know myself
Lock eyes with some haggard dirty voluptuous brown just planted beside me
The day is young, let's get out of here,
I said.

Sometimes

Sometimes, you just gotta lose
Without a why or any clues
The castle don't always shield the king
The sun might rise but you don't hear a thing

Sometimes, you just gotta lose
Can't help but fight, then scratch and bruise
Walk away, and when your back is turned
You realize, not a damn thing earned

Sometimes, you just gotta lose
This world of sin you may refuse
But it can refuse you too, you know
Down on your luck, not a buck to show

Sometimes, you just gotta lose
Get cut off at the shortened fuse
Just when you're about to reach a spark
The plug is pulled and it all goes dark

Sometimes, you just gotta lose
So stand back up on those scuffed shoes
Play the blues, the folk and come what may
Pray you'll be here to dance one more day

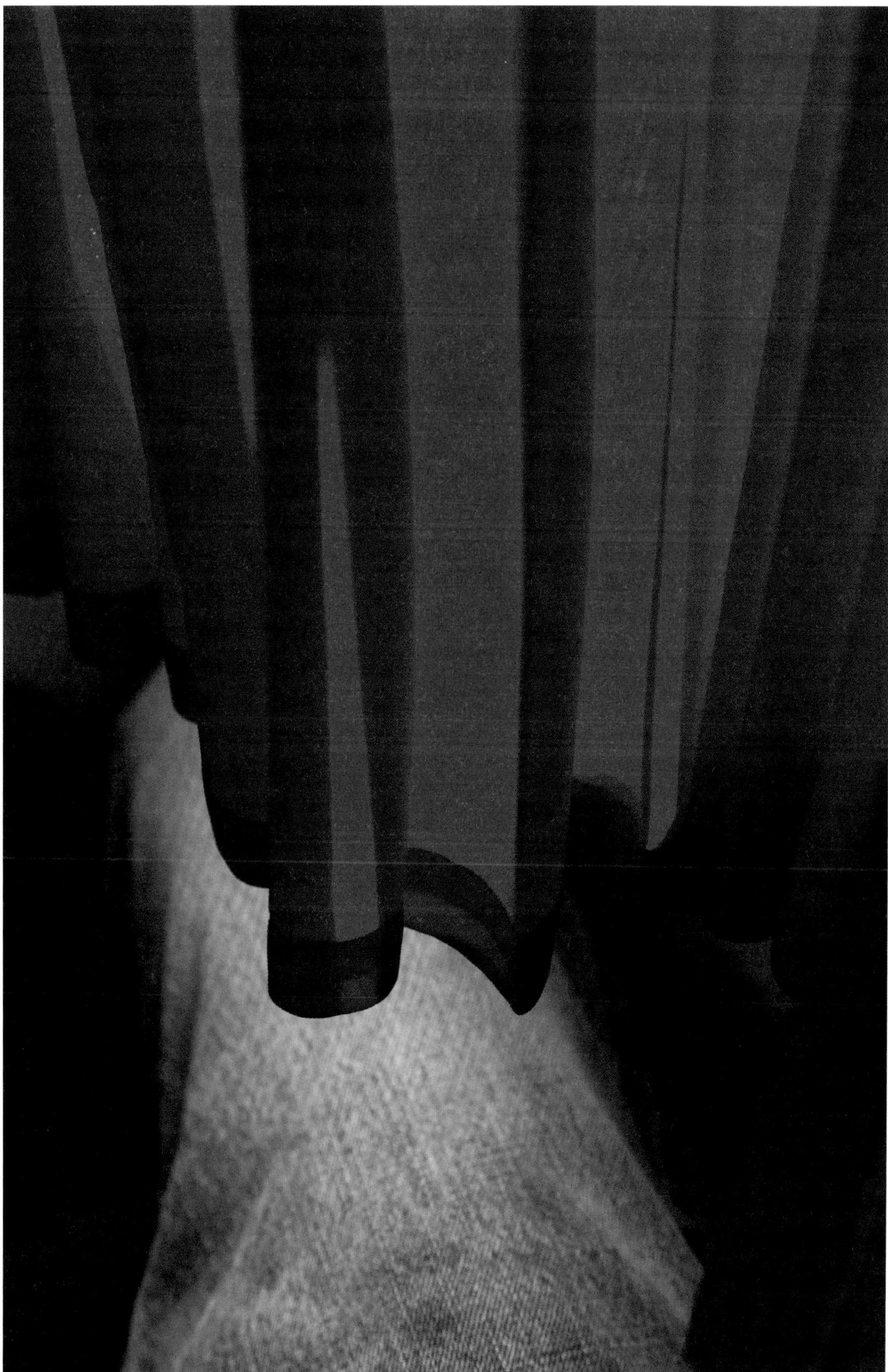

An Ode to Hong Kong No. 3

One midnight, as I had trouble sleeping
My thoughts drifted from sheep to the year of grade four
That concrete, unsafe soccer field on the top floor of school
Where I'd spend my mornings and lunches picking cherries by the goal
Remembered a friend of mine, his name was Willie
I called him Hutch
For some reason that nobody, even I, remembers.
He was an interesting kid, Hutch
Even at that unconscious age
He had a certain adult glimmer to him
Waiting to be unleashed
The only possible trigger would be age
And there'd be no other thing that could set it off
But time.
Hutch, he would say dirty things
Casually slap a girl's ass
Had a weird habit of crossing his legs
That few boys do at that age.
And boy, could he dance.
Like somebody set a firecracker to the seat of Mick Jagger's pants.
The kids are alright,
For they're not so young after all, I guess.
Wonder what happened to Hutch,
Nobody has heard or seen from him since

It's almost like
He just disappeared
Along with everybody else.

A Portrait of Abandon

I once heard about a place
Somewhere
Where a slithering river runs
In the color of snake shaped murk
Flanked by swampy grass
Behind which lie feline-like eyes
Surveying each and all who pass.

Here the smells are exotic and unknowable
Yet carry an alluring waft
Potent in power and persuasion
As if guiding the traveler
To a destination
An entire lifetime has been leading to.

The path of slow, mud baked turf
Carries a variety of footprints
Each pair part of a sensuous portrait
To which the imagination is drawn to picture
Valleys, angles and curves
On a vast uncharted forward that is still blank.

The midst of this Amazonian haze
Remains a muddled, mysterious maze
Seems count has been lost on the ways
Attempted into the Bolivian oblivion
Many a hunter has entered the wild
With very few making the trip back.

Of those who do,
Not a single could explain
Exactly what panned out
During those feverish,
Dream-like jungle days.

2010

Offspring

They broke us up, those sorry kids
All they can do is whine and bitch
Reminds us just of times we did
Burying them leaves us no ditch

What of their future selves will be
Give birth to seed to seal the deal?
They'll kill them too with misery
Serves them right for ungrateful squeals

For now let's drink to toast our plan
The next time I knock you up then
You'll know to go call up the man
Remove the thing before it's been

2012

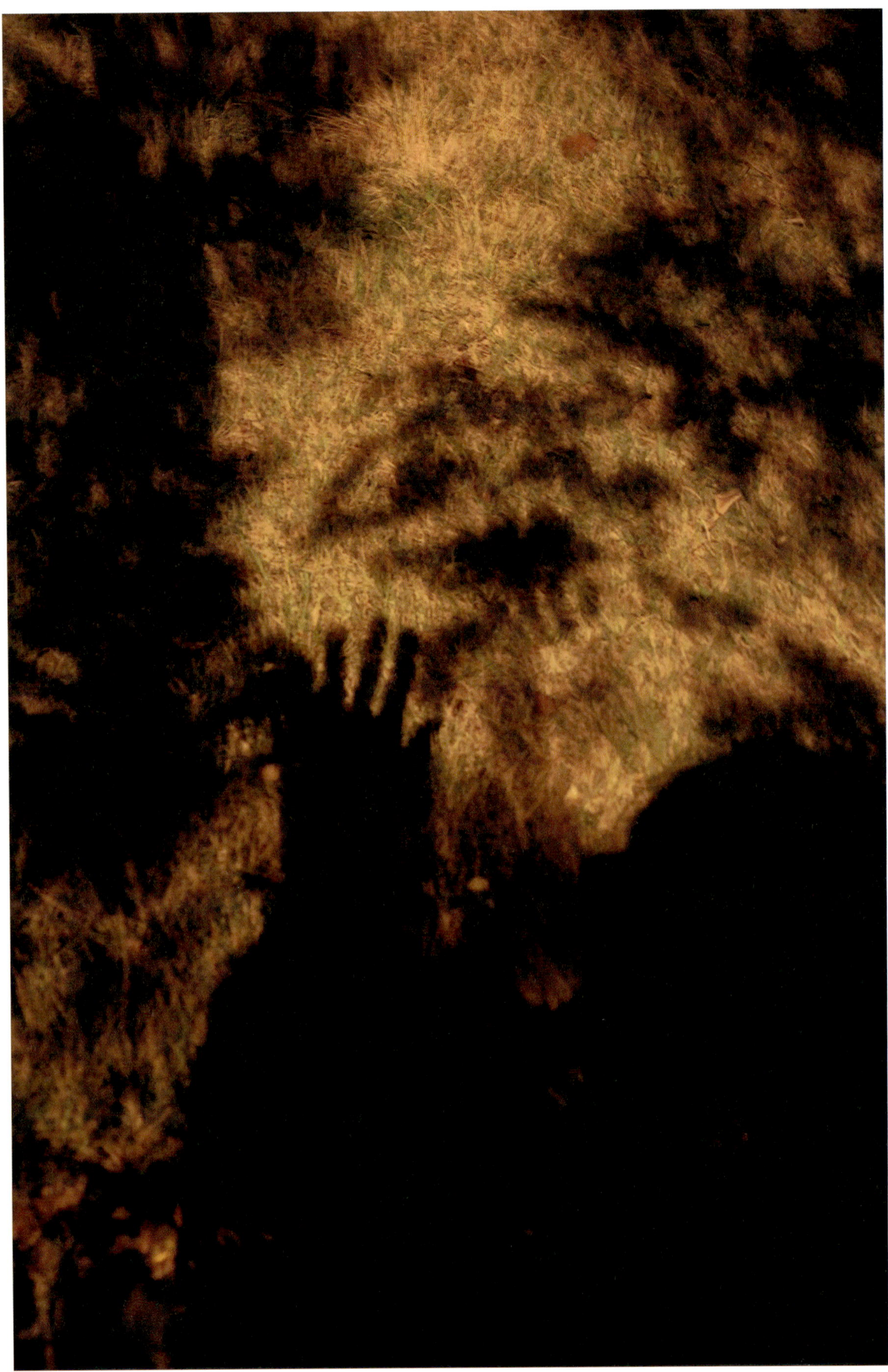

The Passenger [2]

How easy it is to lose sight
Of where these racks lead, like
A bird tucking into a skyline,
Even as one is aware of the fact
That the finished plastic cups
Will do just as well in the absence
Of clock or calendar; nobody
Has taken the seat across as of now.
The shifting views beyond the glass
Are faceless despite their competing
Claims to degrees of irresolution;
Surely a flash of ruptured expanse
Is no substitute for the chiaroscuro
of distinguishable day and night.
Here is where memory comes
To languish in grey compartments
Filled with containers carrying
Various shades of everything
Except their points of origin, all
Of them approaching a wide and empty sea.

Relapse

From a point in the abyss a streak
Of light shoots its way to the beginning
For its second blossom, a cloudlike glow
Emanating fumes fashioned by the stuff
That gives birth to dreams in the human
river; pink pulsations occur deep where
One has been dormant for too long,
The dilation of two pupils merely
A tautological response to instinct,
Resurrecting what was buried but not hidden.

Theme Week

That second week of school we invented
Blackboards on which we would screech
And scrawl our way from one end to
The other, and it felt good, this
Momentary sense of total freedom
And abandonment from orthodoxy,
Like edging towards a lake, naked,
Not aware that there was anyone nearby
Watching. We could write in a language
That couldn't possibly exist, its letters
Elusive and impenetrable, a kind of code
Derived from myths born in the playground,
Something only we knew about.
As the afternoons progressed, the marks left
Increased in their urgency, filled
With the sad knowledge that other things
In the world were waiting, that soon
These surfaces available to us
Would have to be taken down,
The years resuming in dispassionate agency.
By Friday, what was written and erased
Took on a filmic patina of heroic scale,
Monumental for its innocence and absence,
A testament to worlds found, then lost.

Part-time Job

Instances of routine seem
As impossible as a life lived
In full-on entropy. Breaks
Are often and well-deserved;
The day roars past the clouds.
With only the severity of light
Striking the building across
As my clock, I keep watch
For that god-given intersection
When a single panel projects
A beam so complete, I feel all
Must be right again, as I turn
My back on a window of perfection.

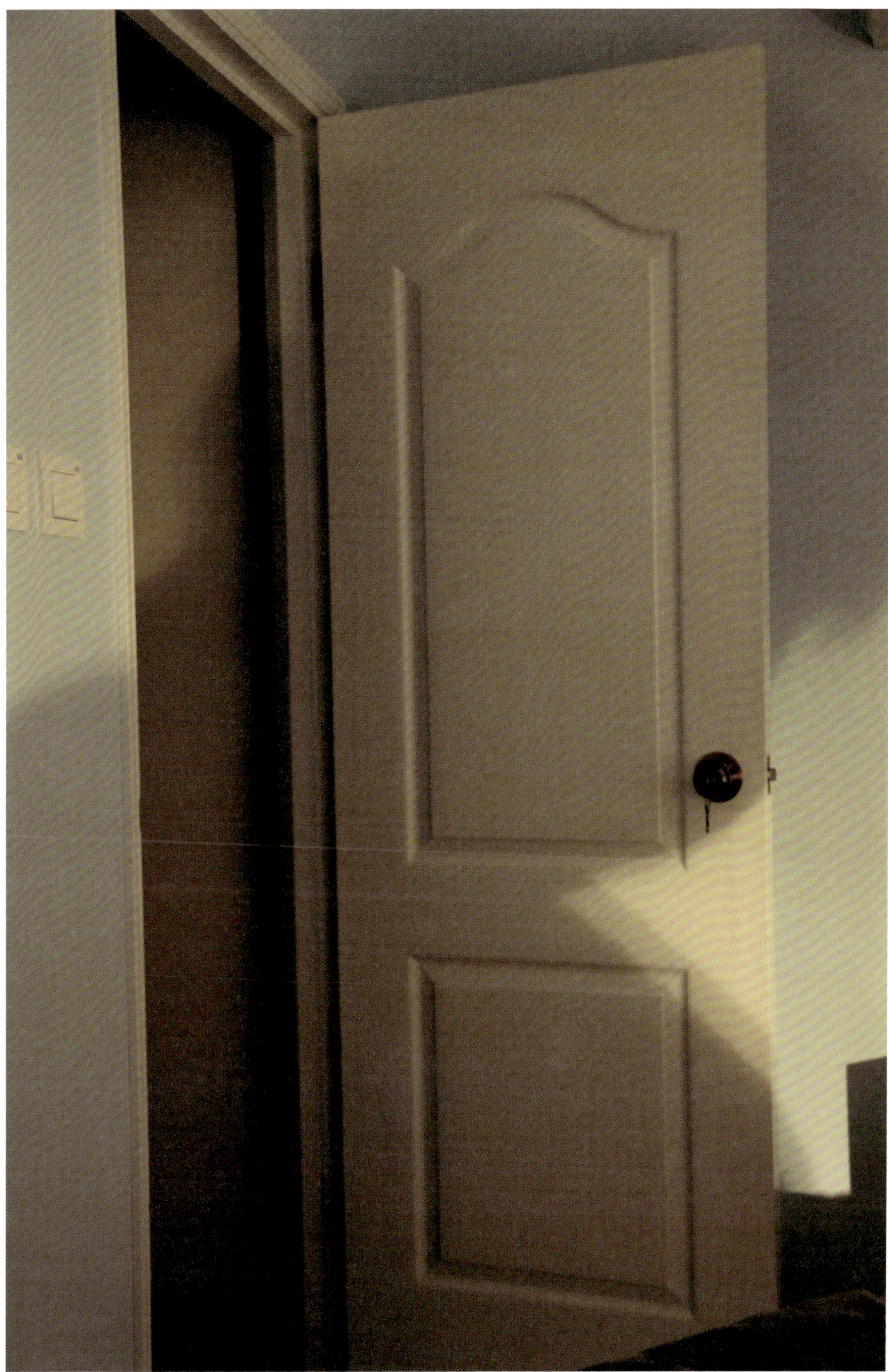

The Killer's Soliloquy

Give me your daughter's irises, so I can dip them
In the kitchen's blood as a requiem for my remorse.
Save me the trouble of counting
Imaginary stars in a prison cell.
The forecast for tomorrow all across
This planet is saturnine, so tell me, doctor.
How do I cope with another book of sorrows
Placed on my front porch?
The rent is due in a couple days
And I can't stand having my shadow evicted.
The sky is full of options. Do I really need
To depend upon a coin to know one's fate?

Normandy

The brain is often like a battlefield
Strewn with so many dead toy soldiers
And letters to women and children
Who will never be seen, again or
For the first time, and blades
Of grass that weep for the flowers
Lying face down in the sand, perhaps
A watch stuck at four fifteen
In the afternoon forever, and mother
Calls your name out loud
From behind, louder again
Now, "Did you hear what
I said? Billy your dinner's ready!"

Beckett

In the vast room
He sat alone
In front of the painting
In silence
And after a while
He let out a sigh.

Paradise

The silver spoon
Lies
At the foot of the door
Untouched
By the shards of broken glass
Surrounding it.
Just another day
On Southside
Of paradise.

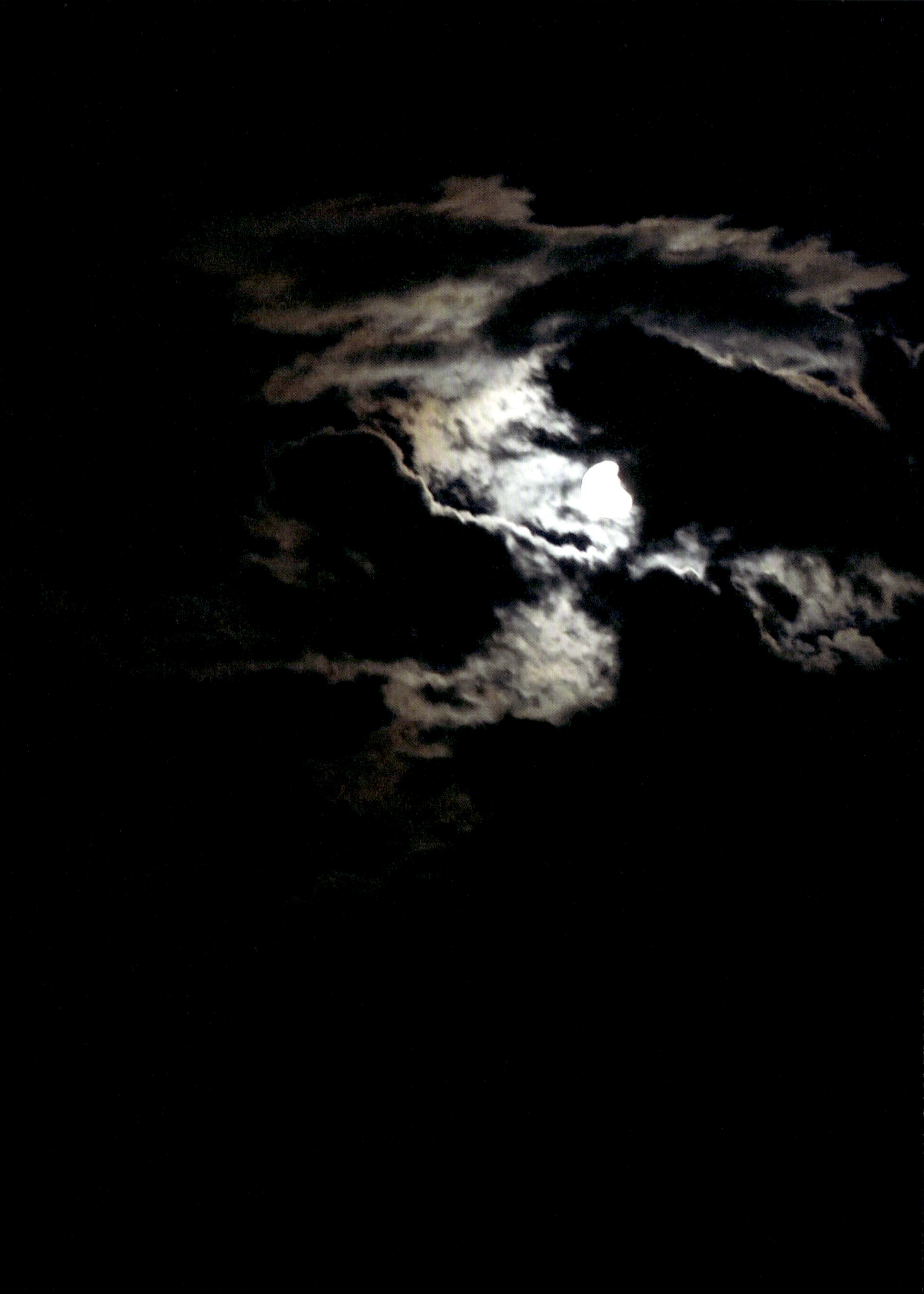

Armageddon Watchers

The sky looked unusually normal considering
what was scheduled for a few hours from
here, as they sat in his father's pickup
he could not help but think of how
absurd the whole thing seemed
yet the right string of words
could not quite hold hands
and leap past his breath
to give the present
tense resonance.

The man pulls
up to the station
telling his son to go
in for two sodas and a
juicy fruit pack, only for
today, he says to himself, so
it will be, when he sees the boy
skipping back out a door held open
he then drifts off the face frozen halfway
between peace and closer still towards regret.

She lets him kiss her where he said he wanted
feeling without much pleasure or resistance
he asks her what's wrong she shakes her
head and pulls him deeper in, stroking
his hair to let him know that the
drop running down her cheek
was not really there but a
skip later she stirs and
says to him not now
not here, not yet.

The Passenger

The man who sits across from me has a stack of paper balanced on a crossed leg and a pencil in his right hand. For three stops it looks as though he is trying to write something, but every time the pencil comes close to meeting the paper it doesn't quite connect, despite his immense concentration. At one point he notices that I've been watching him do this and then turns his complete attention away from the pencil and paper and towards me. I pretend to be looking past him, at my reflection in the window, but this only makes me recognize the ridiculousness of my own appearance. A voice overhead announces that the train will be stalled for several minutes due to an accident up ahead, and sorry for the inconvenience. I shrink in my seat and fill my thoughts with foreign music. The air is thick as the whole car goes silent save for the instruments I force my head to play, and I start to hold my breath. I turn red, then purple, and then even my mental orchestra becomes jangled into blips of noise. I feel the floor dissipate and what must be a holy light penetrates my vision. A warm tingle runs through my body. Someone's hand touches my shoulder, and I know I am ready for salvation.

Inspirado

The polar bear sits
On the fence.
Awaiting judgment;

Nobody
Is watching more anxiously
Than the two red hats
Perched by the bar.

Of all the six million things
That could come from a light bulb,
It happened to be this. What
That means, in a Freudian sense,
Remains unperturbed.

Ecstasy

Their eyes leaned back like irises. "So this," he said, "is what ecstasy feels like." Thumbing the dry sole of her left foot, he had flashbacks of drinking coffee with bubble gum in his mouth, a pleasantly nauseating boat ride to sunny Capri one day in youth, daffodils parked on the asphalt outside Sheridan Shopping Center while a matinee was playing amongst dandelion skirts grazing pressed powder khakis; all the effortless bebop of a back-and-forth in one's rocking chair after a first glimpse into the future. It would be presumptuous to intrude upon this easy, worldless dialogue, but a phone rings, followed by a few rhythmic raps on the door. Not missing a beat, the watchmen pirouette into the sepia-toned valley and make their business felt. Bobby keeps playing on the soundtrack as the trenchcoats hightail Sam and Sue to kingdom come, leaving their little deaths behind like a pair of forgotten siblings.

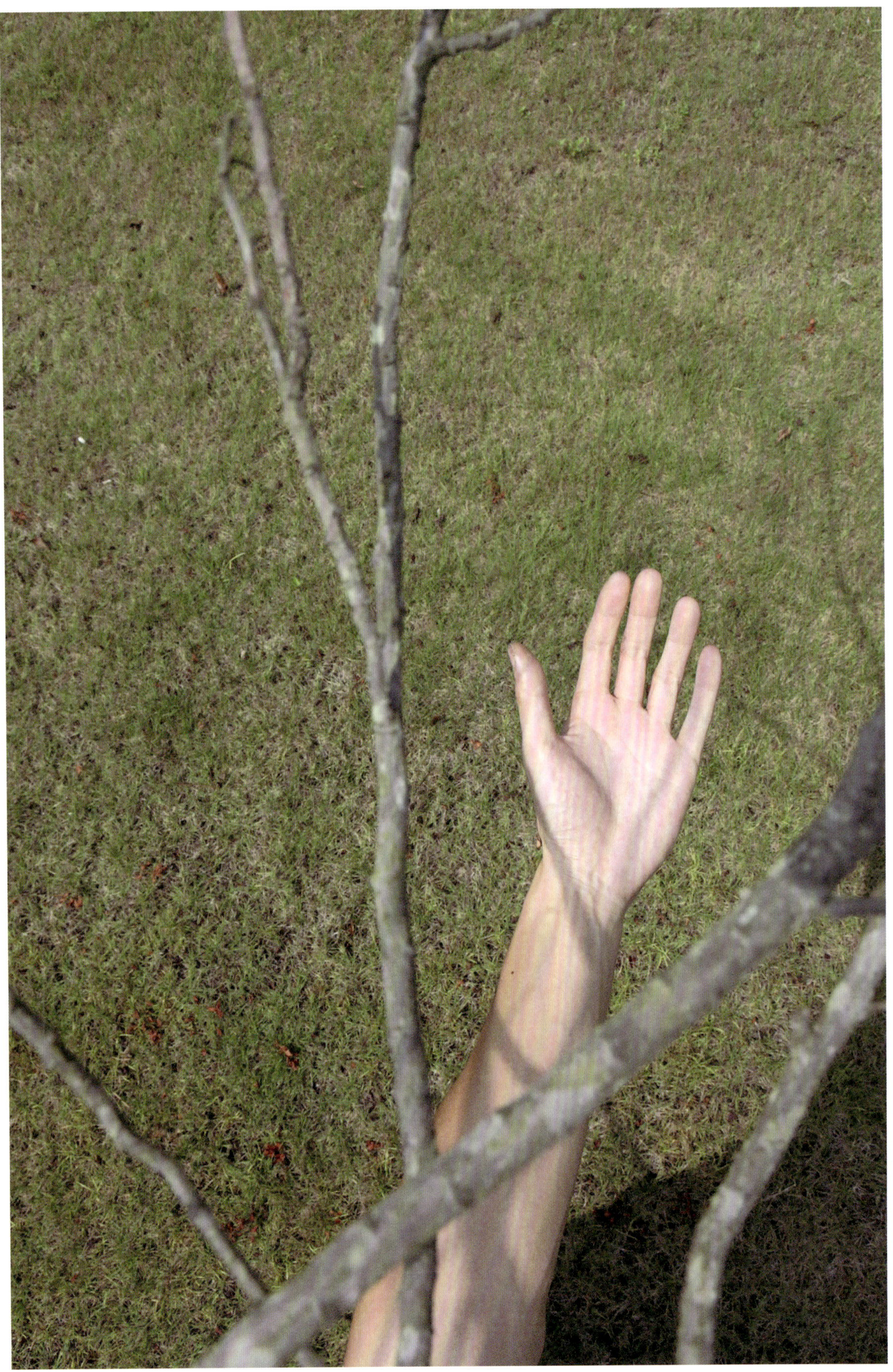

Smoke

How to hold a cigar:
Firm, but gently,
Like a lover.
I read that bit
When I was seventeen,
The year I started smoking.
Those words
Were on my mind
In the back of a taxicab
In Varadero,
Outside the nightclub.
I asked her,
"Are your folks home?"
She ran a finger
Across her neck,
"Dead."
I don't remember
What cigars I smoked that night,
But I remember
The sensation of smoke
Drifting off in the air,
Towards the sea.

The Dinner Party

Glasses shimmered underneath the chandelier by the entrance.
The hostess was surrounded by a group of friends
Listening to her talk about the past.
Her hands moved around the pearls on her necklace
As she wondered why they seemed to be getting fewer.
"Oh, as you get older, that's just how it goes
They're in the back of your mind every now and then,
And you keep meaning to call and make plans for next week,
And the next thing you know—
Decades have gone by!"

Ink Square

The musician looks
Out his window
Into the winter light, and thinks
To himself
That his present position
Was familiar,
Like a certain kind of stranger.

The place was new
And barely furnished,
Yet his first impulse
Had been to hang
The three drawings of squares
Right above the bed.
In this way, overlooking his head
Was black on black on black,
A shield against the silence
And all the things it never said.

Good Ass Job

Even as a boy he took an interest in women
who didn't seem to be interested by much
except shoes and cars, he didn't know them
yet but would wonder if there was perhaps
some room left in there for a rueful star, one
much like himself maybe. then as he got older
he would often go visit department stores
and chat up salesladies in that precocious way
he thought only he could, but never enough
to get a number or anything, besides
that wasn't what he had in mind anyway. guess
he just liked the feeling of getting out there
and learning to ease into things. growing up
in a style that didn't seem peculiar to him,
they found him kind of charming. later on
he went to art school and moved out
of chicago to los angeles and things changed
a bit, some for the better, others not so much.
it's been quite a few years since he sat
by the window writing poems and banging on
hard and flat surfaces alone, some of the

spark wasn't there anymore, same with the
girls. but one time as a kid he saw a car parked
outside the steakhouse and a smart looking man
got out with a pretty doll around his arm
and he thought to himself that's going to be me
one day.

Matters of the Flesh

The first time I bought a tube
Of oil paint,
I ran the few blocks home.
Squeezing Prussian blue
Into the ashtray with anticipation,
I turned on the bathroom sink
To let a few drops in.
The broad brush I also bought
Didn't last very long,
But it did its job
Under the slit of sun
Pecking through the curtains
Three quarters pulled,
A mess of paper everywhere.

2013

Skin

Skin is something to peel back
Layer by layer, fold by fold
Until you are at its core.
Where you may stay as long
As you please, and when you're done
You just seal it back up
Like a package waiting for the next person
To come along, like a message in a bottle.

Breakdown in Broad Daylight

Fanaticism grates on my nerves.
I was on my way to the cinema
When I had to cross the street
At a major intersection
And some Tai Chi cult
Was blocking traffic
With a marching band procession.
By the time I finally made it across
I had five minutes to showtime
And twelve blocks to go.
I left a trail of broken brass and bones
In my wake.
I'm telling you this
Cause nowadays I can't get ANY
Satisfaction in the city
Never mind if the next man don't
Smoke the same brand of cigarettes as me.

Process

Lying in a forlorn alleyway that sticks out
Among old, upscale numbers of residence,
These eight large sheets of paper
Are catching raindrops. A few
Drizzles of ink, and now they're dealing
With chance. The sheets go from off white
To total dark in a flash. I stack them up
And fold the stack in half.
The walk home down to the other end
Of the avenue and around the corner
Leaves a snaking fluid trail
On the pavement, which keeps changing
With every drop. I can only hope
That when the papers have fully dried,
They will reveal light.

Waiting for G

I want you, mouthed the ballerina
Nursing her broken feet at the bottom
Of a gallon bottle. It was midnight
And my vision was getting prickly
From the grotesque, slippery light
Molesting every inch of this abandoned
Warehouse. These sunglasses do nothing.
My doppelganger is sitting across
From me, surrounded by glass,
Still but tenuous. I decide
To play a game. I will ask him
Three questions, one of which
He has to answer correctly, otherwise
I will shoot him. A fair proposition,
Given the circumstances.
What is the meaning of Nebraska, and how
Many birthday candles does it take
To make a t-bone steak look like
A jackass? I flip a coin for no reason
While thinking of an appropriate
Third question. But then he speaks—
Time will tell, my friend, time will tell.

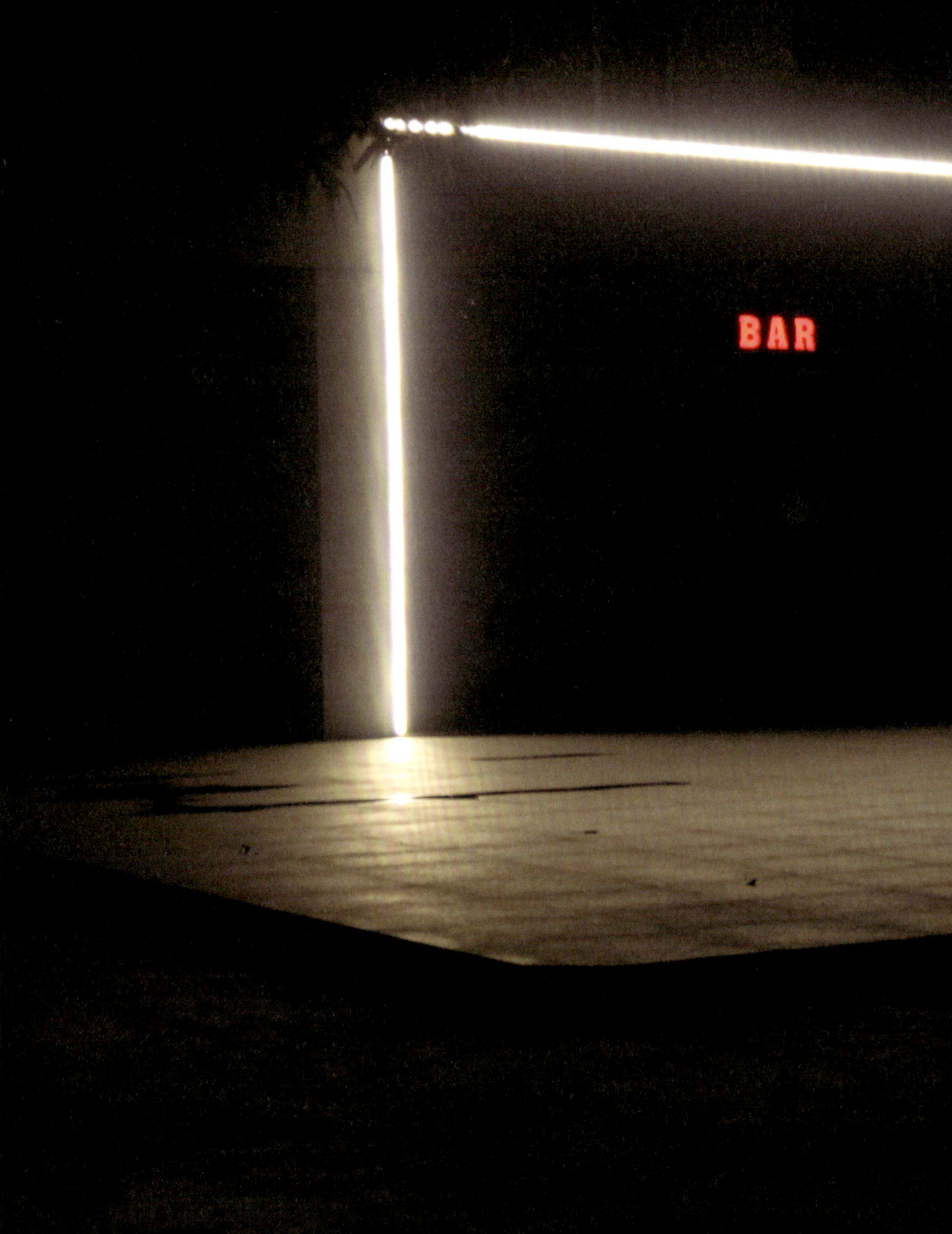
BAR

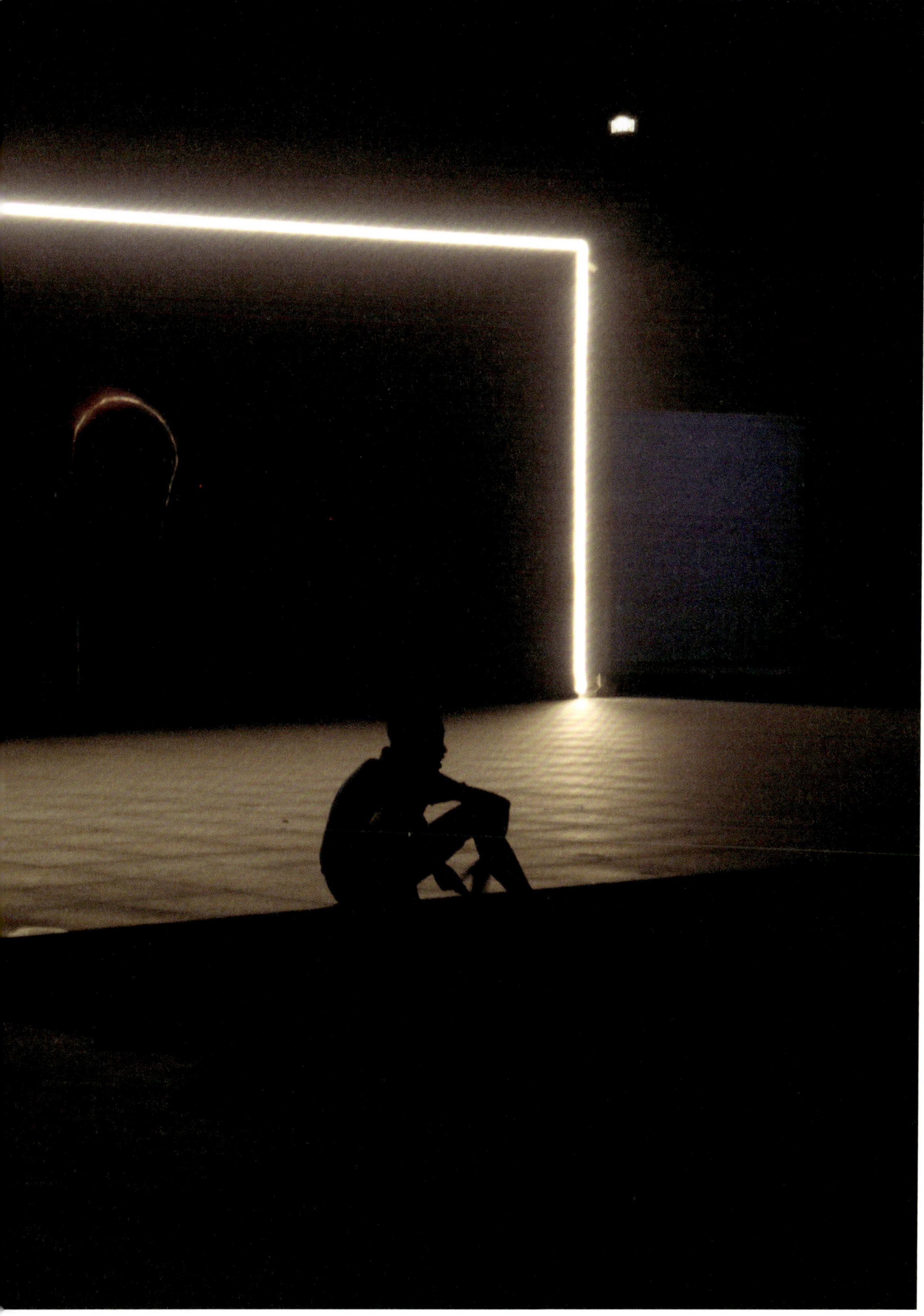

Truth or Consequences, New Mexico

I read somewhere that Bob Dylan
Is good at moving in and out
Of gas stations, diners, and supermarkets
Incognito. I can do that as well, just
As well as Bob can. I am responsible
For my own zeitgeist. I've been writing
My favorite photographer from Japan
A sequence of love poems and have yet
To hear back from her. A friend I saw once
Every few years said to me, exasperated,
"People are just. . .BUSY! You know?"
Yeah, I know. I keep waiting. A job,
A wife, two kids and barbecues
In the backyard is a good idea. But I believe
One idea is just as good as another,
So I think I'll let the sun in and take a nap.
With Karen Carpenter singing me to sleep.
Maybe a butterfly will fly through the window

Matinee

I saw you in a photo
From nine years ago
At an after party for the Globes
And the man with a hand
Holding a champagne flute,
The other behind your neck
Puts me beyond language.
I wake up late the next afternoon
To find it raining, and arrive just
In time to watch you leave the bedroom.

A History of Violence

Have you been experiencing headaches
When you hear music in elevators?
I have not set foot in an elevator in ten years,
Sir. Do you fantasize about special relations
With married women? I have no interest
In any bond of a sexual nature, sir.
You are walking down the street
And see a hundred dollar bill out in the open;
What do you do? I do not believe
In lunch and a pair of jeans both for free, sir.
Take a look at this ink drawing. What
Do you see? I see a biomorphic abstraction
Open to any number of interpretations,
But ultimately residing in a material realm
Beyond the grasp of language, sir.
Oh fuck you. Excuse me, sir?
I was there. Do you remember the night
When you were five, and your parents
Told you to hide in the closet, and then
You heard some noise, gunshots,
And when you came out they were both dead?
I made you an orphan. I'm here now,
Old and unarmed. Is there anything
You want to say or do to me, you cockroach?

Jealousy

I am deep in the library, alone.
In the way one is, or can be,
Alone on a strange planet. My girlfriend
Is probably getting ready
To go to church at this moment.
I feel no sense of trespass
As I walk with assurance
And determination to my target:
I reach a far-off section
And there it is—I pull out
The thin blue volume
Written by the French lady,
A book which I learned
Contains the word 'onanism'
Time and time again.
I hold the book in both hands.
I do not want to move.

Where I Found Myself

It was near the end of the longest
Summer day as I stepped
Into the phone booth to make a call
That shouldn't have taken very long.
As I slid the door shut,
I realized that I have walked into
A house where every person who has used
This phone is in the middle
Of a party. It seems that dessert
Has already been served, and the guests
Are now drinking in the living room.
I look down to make sure my fly is not
Undone. Martha from 4:30 PM
On this day exactly a year ago
Invites me to a ménage a trois
In the master bedroom
With an unnamed tomboy
Who used the phone this morning.
I politely decline. Never having
Been good at small talk,
I light a Winston to keep my hands busy,
And then a man who looks like
My father comes up to me and says,
"My name is Winston!" After
A weak handshake, we look ruefully
At a Van Gogh on the wall
That has turned mostly grey.
I go up to the second floor,
Walking the creaky corridor
And hear the sounds of people

Fucking everywhere. The noise
And decay of this place
Is too much to bear. Halfway back down
The stairwell, I catch a mother in the corner
Who could not have been older
Than my younger sister
Breast feeding her infant,
While her older daughter
Is staring into deep space
With a bright red lollipop.
I am watching the scene, transfixed, until
I hear a police car siren getting closer
And remembered our Dirty Harry date
So I leave quickly without saying goodbye
And start running as fast as I can
To the cinema.

The Visitor

In the hour you were born,
I kept passing by, like raindrops
Outside an April window.

The day you took the hand
Of your bride, I threw a spare coin
Into the plaza fountain.

It is almost night
As I walk towards you now
Across forest and sky
With tears in my blood.

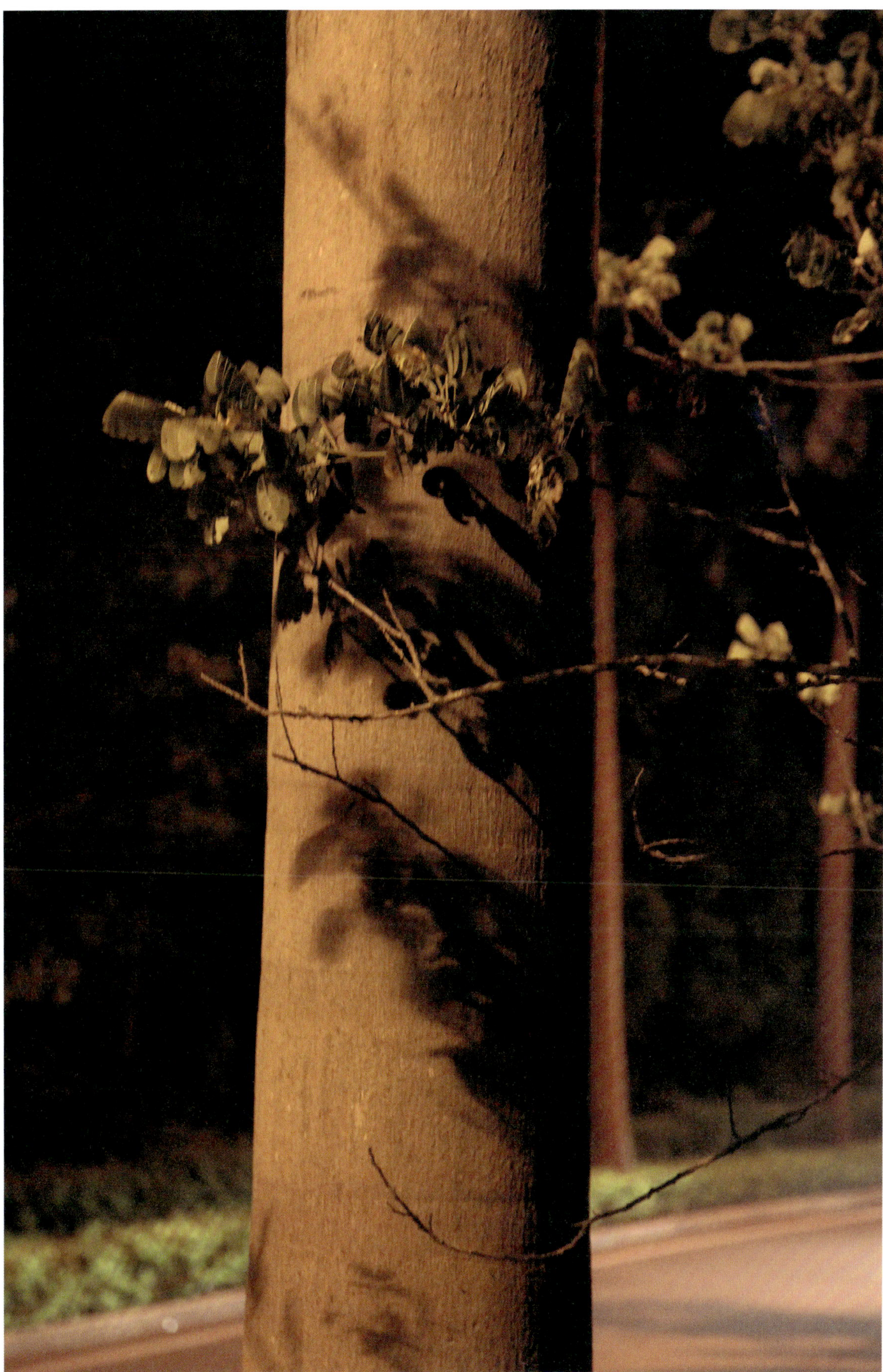

Vacuum

In the northernmost point of China, where the nation is bordered by Russia and the moon, there is an apartment building of unspeakable architecture that is being guarded solely by a gaunt man who has forgotten his age. The man wears a pale blue security uniform that hangs off his body the way water falls from a bucket. There are no calendars here, and each unit contains neither door nor window. The inhabitants, sealed into their rooms by a facade of cement and ivory, pass the time by writing poetry on the walls with their fingertips, without sorrow, without hope, the words coming from a language that does not exist.

Oil

Oil does the body a whole lot
Of good. Around the collarbone,
Behind the knees, on a cracked out jaw.
Hands, feet, wrists, thighs, unwatching the game
On television. A box of Kleenex, silk
Blue shorts; is anybody keeping score?

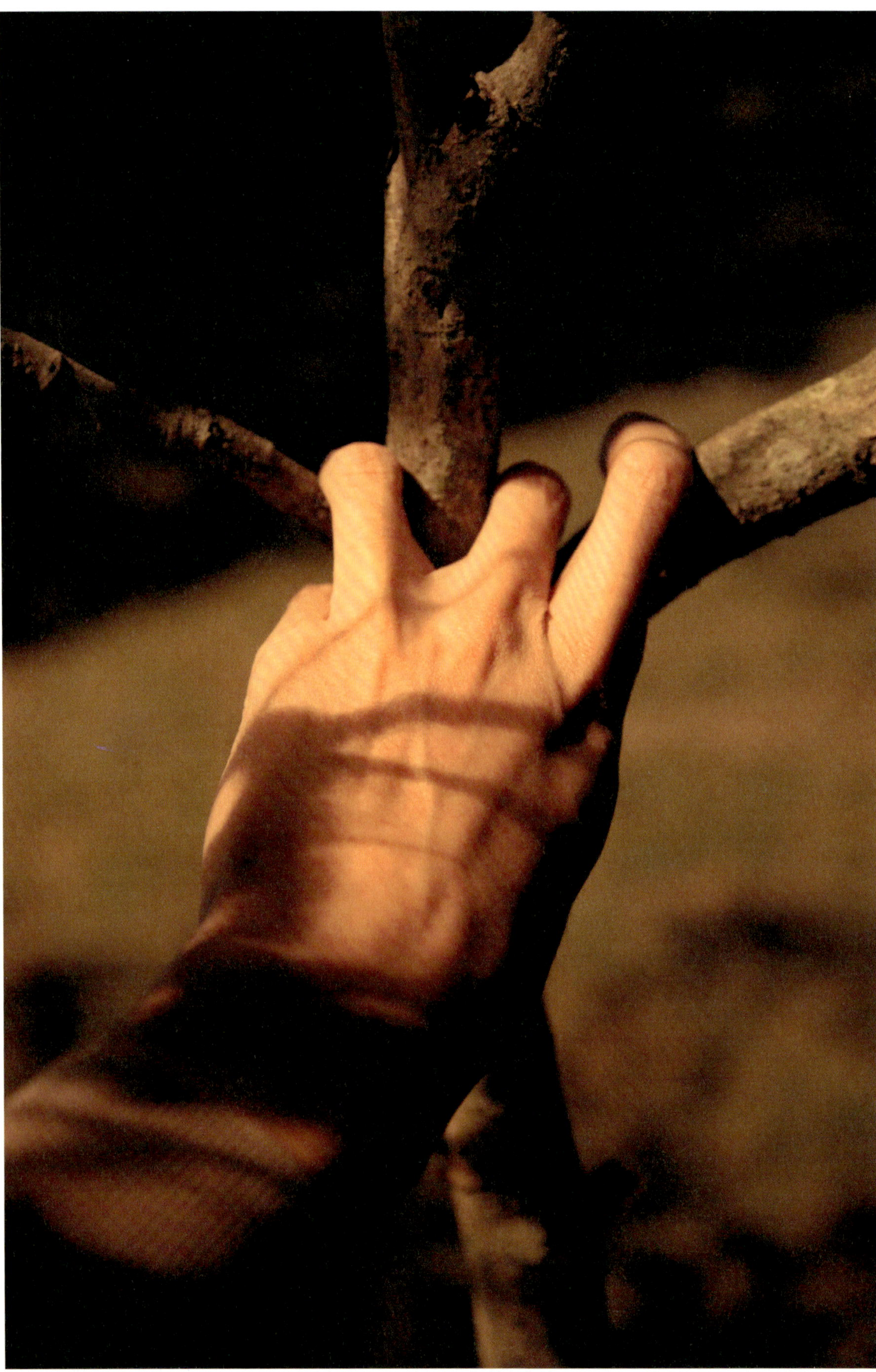

Dictation

A shy wind is bidding the desert farewell as my wife and I tuck into
another dinner of beans and rice. Our silence echoes the landscape
surrounding us. I have been having trouble writing since we arrived, and
our sleep has not fared much better. After I finish my plate, I get up
without a word and begin walking. I go on until the campfire from where
I started has become nothing, and I penetrate the vague darkness of my
path without awe or fear. I take off my clothes. Any sense of time has
passed, along with place, but at a point I stop to look down, and see a void
where I feel that my cock is hard. I get on my knees to flatten a patch of
sand, and then put the crown of my head on it, using my arms for support
to slowly raise my legs until they pointed towards the sky. In this position,
I waited to meet the sun.

Saturday Afternoon

I stare at the table in front of me, grey,
Bloodless now. I reach under my chair
For the miracle whip, and empty
What's left of the jar onto the table.
By the sink is a weathered plastic bag
Containing oil and acrylic paint tubes
In various stages of freshness. One by one,
I squirt what remains of them onto
The table: Burnt sienna, perylene black,
Naples yellow, Prussian blue, Hooker's green
And flesh tint. I open the refrigerator
To find a week old shank and cherry jam
Sharing the space with nothing else.
The jam is dumped onto the table
And spread even with a butcher's knife.
I unseal the meat and rub it around
The growing, ineffable mixture. The table's
Surface takes on an otherworldly glow.
I go down into the basement to look
For anything else that would be of use.
There are gallons of water and turpentine
Which I haul up towards the room
And pour with love and rage onto the table,
Into the sink, the fridge, against the battered
Door. I feel incomplete but am growing tired,
So I lie down on the cold, wet floor and watch
A fly skirting the ceiling. The telephone rings.

Once

A pigeon arrives at my doorstep
And the smell of chestnuts come to mind.
The pigeon is fat and not unlovely.
She looks up at me with the haunted eyes
Of a songstress who is chained to her bed
Even when she is flying over Lake Erie.
Two tears are swimming their way up
My throat as I tell the bird, "Oh we could
Have flown together through the forest once.
Will you sing me one last song
For what might have been, my love?"

Night Poem

I am standing on a balcony
In a staring contest with the lady
On the moon. A galaxy of ants
Are making their way in and out
Of my eyes, but I refuse to blink.
I blink. The moon is no longer there.

The Room

Close your eyes and describe to me
What you see. I see a room full
Of nothing. Would you like to stay
There for the night? Yes, I would like
To lie down here and fall asleep.

Station

No one gets out of here alive—
Written in a parched red on green tiles.
I read the line for longer than
I should. I walk out the door
Without washing my hands, thinking,
Where are you now?
Where are you now?

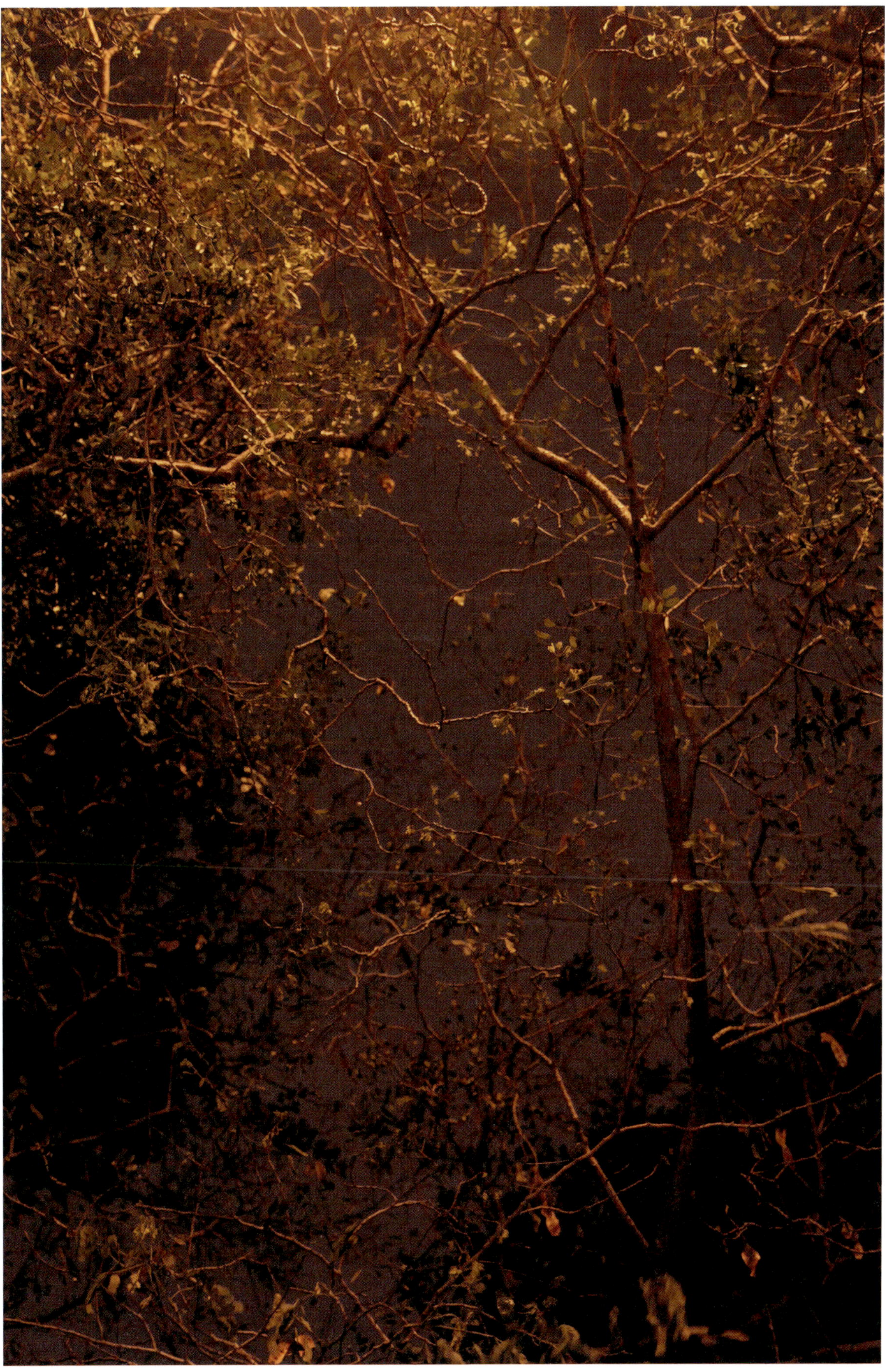

Poem for de Kooning

This poem could be about a river,
A cat, or a door. It could be speaking of
The summer of your youth, spent
Lying in a yellow patch, looking up
And not caring much for the difference
Between very far away and right here,
Then and now, father and mother.
The poem can be many things
Depending on who you are.
I know what it is to me, and I know
How water and the sun feel
Through my lingers on an August afternoon.

Winter Scene

A mouse trapped in an hourglass, still, looks
At me, or is it the other way around?
The wood beneath my soles is turning
To a leaden sand. Inside my boots
I can feel the passing minutes dissolving
Into the pores of my skin, through my bones
And then shivering up the spine
With increasing ecstasy, and I let out
A sound that is small but strange
Beyond description. What has fallen
Upon this house? I know better than to ask
Out loud, even if the place is empty
Save for me and the creature. The wind
That blows outside the night has ears,
After all.

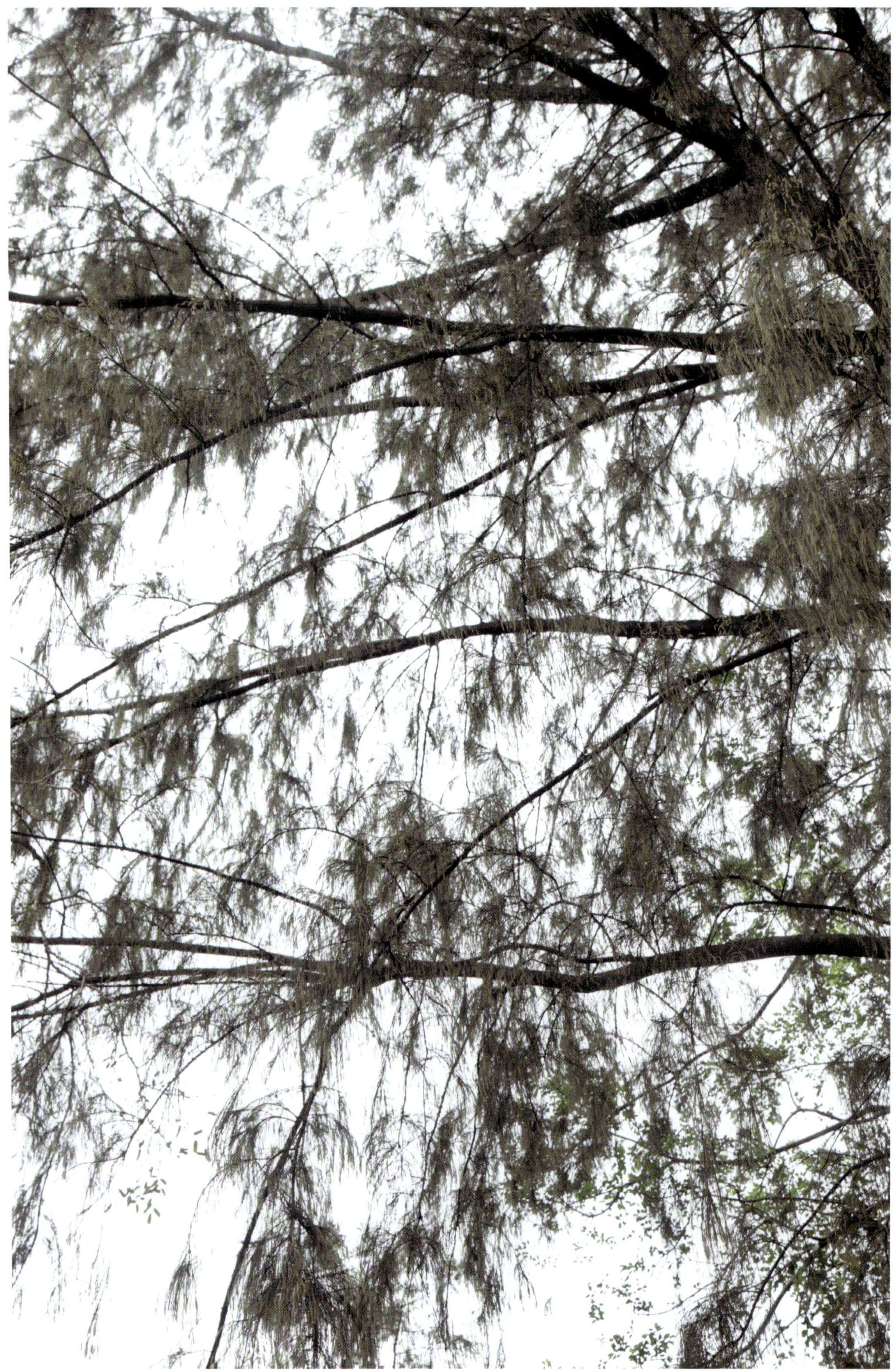

Bad Education

You say you
Know a thing
Or two, but all
I can absorb
Is your knees
On that floor
With no carpet.
Your pale fingernails
Tied like shoelaces. I look
Outside and see
Drunk, pathetic sky.
Phallus-shaped cloud
Heading in our direction.
The girl in an old sweat-
Shirt I've been meaning
To ask out but won't
Opens the window.
What now?

Untitled

It is late, and the children
Of thunder are gathering
Around a fire somewhere
In the distance, in a place
Where you are not.
You have lust in your bones
And you want anarchy;
You want to disrobe
Yourself of pride the way
Your eye undresses
A woman on the subway
Or in a photograph.
You understand that all
That remains of heaven
Is a memory, and that love
Knows silence as a river
Through the woods knows blood.

The Island

Whoever said that no man
Is an island is a fool, for are you not
At this moment wet and stranded
Among my outer wreckage,
Praying for the sting of salt to go away?

Where They Came From

I used to think that clowns all came
From out of the same cave, a cave
Whose mouth was very wide, and very high.
They sprang from a nothing
Located deep inside the cave's belly
Already fully formed, with bright honking noses
And wearing their candy colored,
Balloon-bottom clown uniforms, they walked
Into the world single-file, down to a beach
Where big pink boats were waiting
To take them across a white, weightless sea
And drop them off at any place
That contained childhood, so that they
Could carry out their purpose
And bring laughter where
There might be sadness and fear.
Then one day I saw a clown
Come out of a car with my mother,
Who never wore lipstick, but her smile
Was a shade of red I had never seen before.
At that moment I learned that clowns just came
From the same place as you and me.

Far

It was around ten in the morning
When I stopped by the cart
To buy a soda. The man
Gave me my can and said
To me, in his best English,
"I have high hopes for you.
My friend, you will go far!"
I thanked him. He did not know
That I was already far. I looked up
Towards the Venetian sky, squinting
Past a pair of birds, and waited
For someone to call my name.

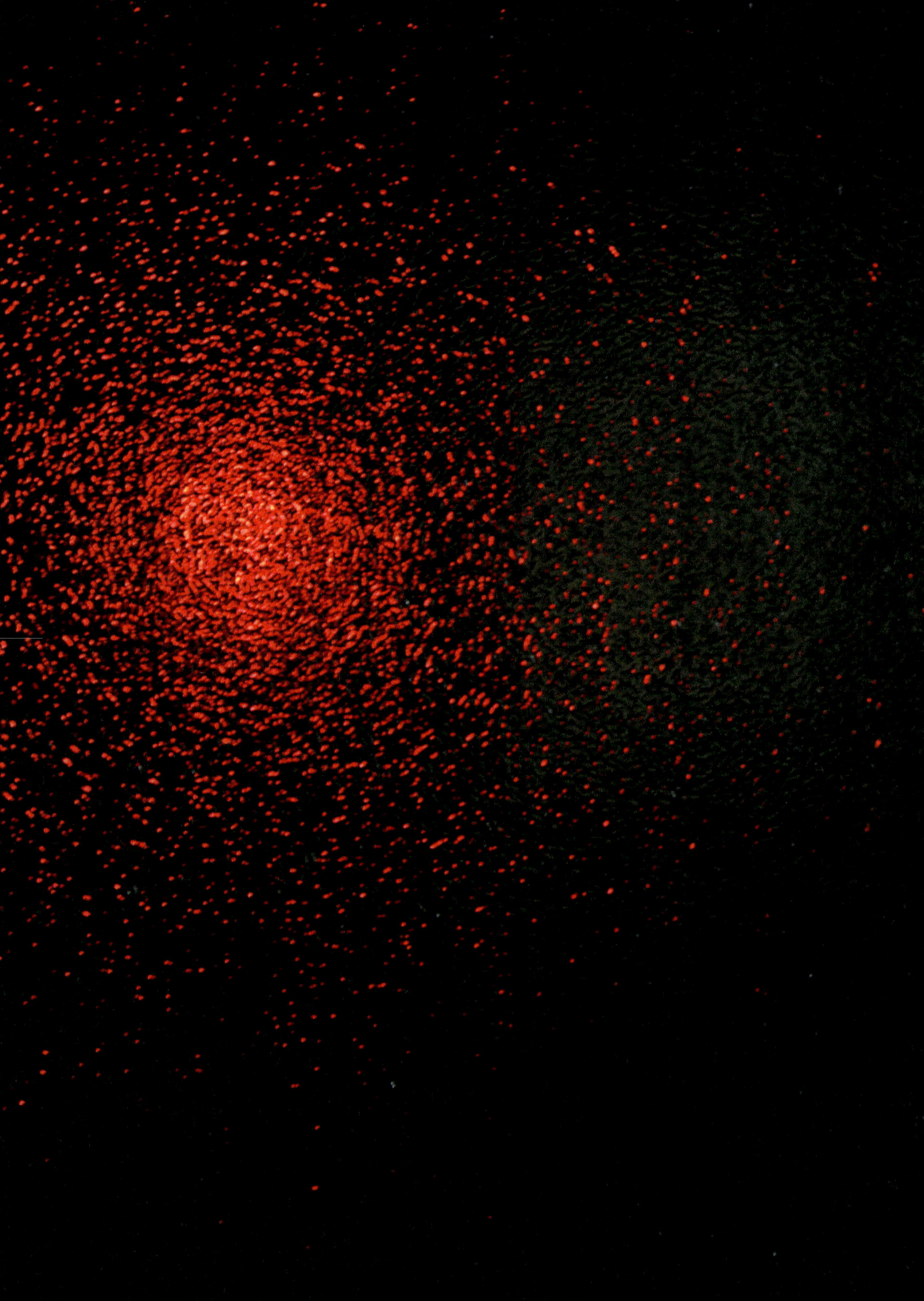

My Wallet

There is a folded napkin I carry
In my wallet; on it is the only kiss
I've ever received. Since I'm always broke,
My few friends are always teasing
Me about why I even need to own
A wallet. "You have no credit, hardly
Any loose change—surely just
Your pockets will do!" Untrue, I say.
I carry a poem in there, a moment suspended
Between leather folds; I'm the richest man
You'll ever know! Not knowing
What it was like to love, they shrugged.
Not knowing what it was like to have,
I laughed.

Ashes

To think, every speck of ash you come
Across in this life may once have been
Somebody's nose, a house
For a family of three or a field
Under the Cuban sun—if I knew
Every secret that came in the color grey,
I would prefer to have my lips sealed
For five thousand years as a Sphinx
Rather than be a man who has to put on
His hat and coat in order to go to work today.

They're Playing Our Song Again

Beige room, thoughts adrift
In an invisible sea. The radio hits
The first few notes which come out
Like the sun from a blanket of ocean
And then I'm falling down our song again—
"My cherie amour. . ."—I am now a body
Hurling through the center
Of a spiral staircase. It's November
And raining, and you are probably at work
While I write this, thinking of me
Thinking of you. What are the chances
Of finding the rest of your life
Outside a poetry reading, anyway?

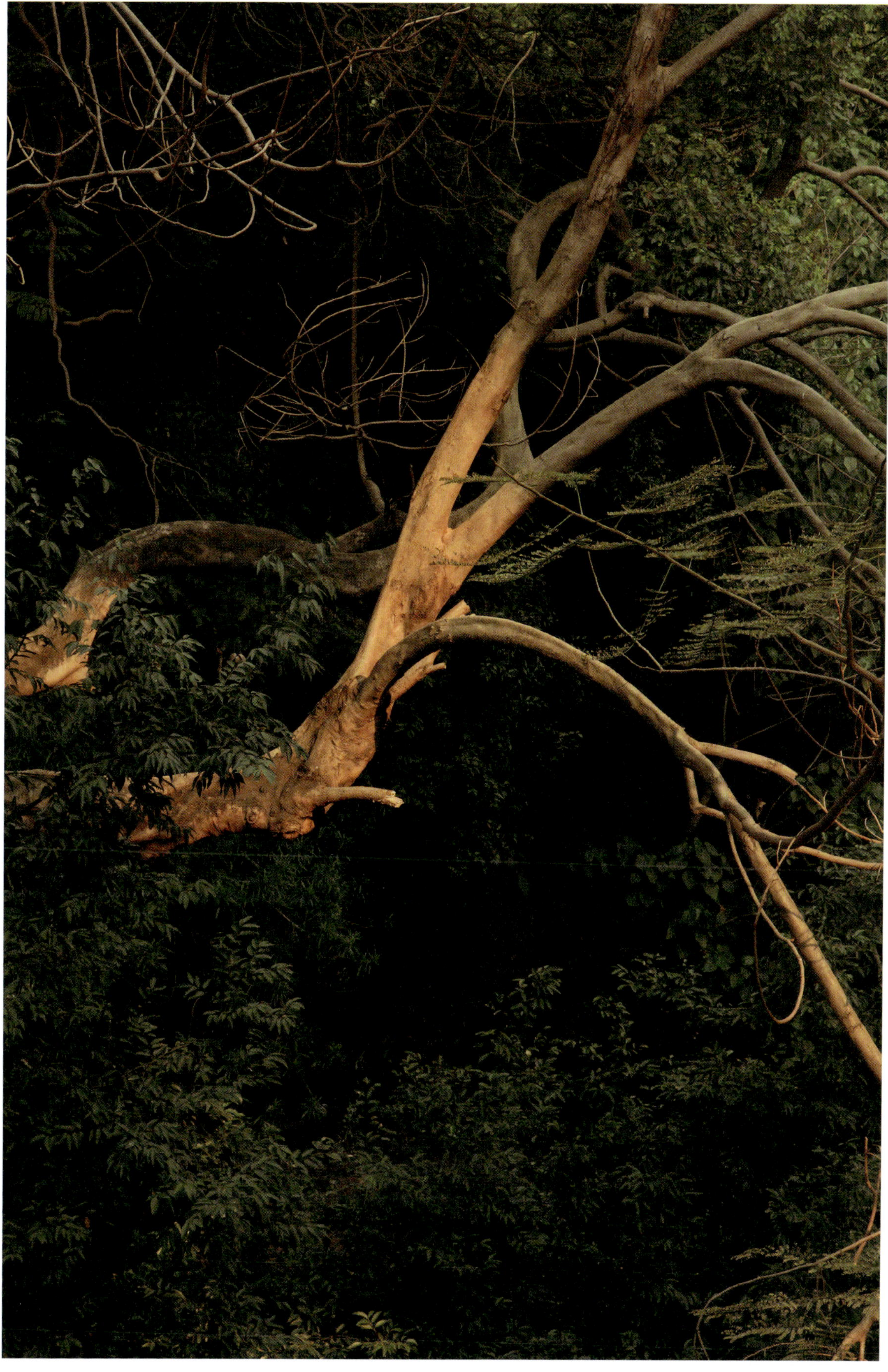

Late Afternoon

The man was down to his last few bites
In this world, and how fitting it seemed
That the last thing his teeth should sink into
Was a peach. The executioner watches
With a golden film undulating in his eyes,
"How did that taste, my friend?"
"You will never know, my friend. Never."

The Lesson

Do as I tell you, ageless child,
And dip the tip of your brush in the days-old
Ink, which must feel more like molasses now,
And draw a circle on the page, swiftly,
With your eyes closed. Then open
Your ears, and your heart, and the rest
Of your internal organs, but not the eyes,
Never the eyes. Do you hear your circle
Speaking? There is nothing perfect
About perfection. What is that shape,
Not fully known but present, saying
To you? Reciting a poem about the dreams
That forests have when they are asleep?
Or perhaps describing what it felt like
To be a stone impregnating the first ocean
That would then give birth to your mother.
The circle, still in front of you, unseen,
Agape, might not even be saying
Anything resembling a word, instead
Breathing a wind that blows like no breeze
At all, but when it touches your skin,
You will become awake in every pore
To your lawless impermanence.
This is the first step.

First Day of School

Sing, my dear boy, for the stars
Missing your mother on this
Rainy morning. Sing for your father's shoes;
He will leave home after breakfast, barefoot,
To go to France to be a king
& won't be coming home for supper
Tonight. Sing as loud as you can
Until you throw up, so that you will learn
Freedom sometimes doesn't taste
Like cotton candy on the seat
Of a Ferris wheel. Sing for the puddles,
The huddles, sing for your bulging eyes
And swimming trunks, soon enough
You'll be a man, and I an even older one.
Come sit on my lap and sing
Until it's dark again, and you want to fall
Asleep, and when you are dreaming,
I will come sit in yours
And tell you everything I know
About a faraway country built
Out of nothing but air. I lived there
When I was your age.
Everyone around me was always laughing.

Poem for Bob Dylan

I've forgotten what city I'm in today.
I just know that it's cold; the day or month
Does not even matter, and why
Should it, when the only thing I need
To know about right now is that
The pavement is the same color
As my shoes are the same color
As the wind making love to every inch
Of my face, everything as one,
The world's sound and silence soaking
Like a sponge in my veins. I say
To the air before me: go on now,
Child of motherless grace.
Nevermind where, just walk.

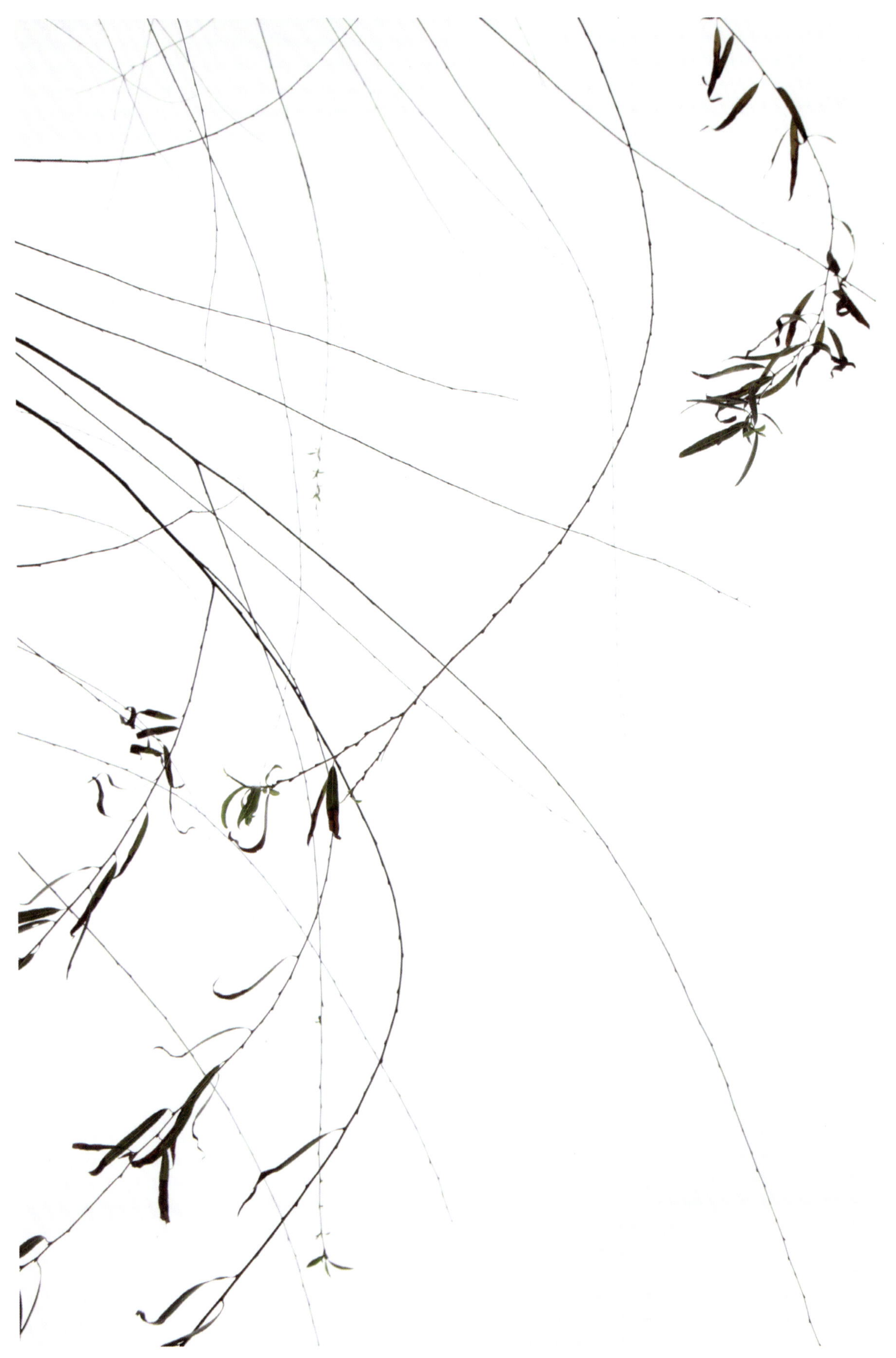

The Other Side

The clouds are singing
With their skirts up
Mountains in the distance
Drinking from the river like giant
Camels after a very long walk
But it's just my brain being silly
I know they have no legs
And haven't budged
In thousands of years, maybe more
They must be open to anything
At this point, and what about
The lustful grass sucking
The toes of those ticklish trees
Everything outside this window
So beautiful the sun wants to cry
So what am I still in bed for
I'm already naked
Under these sheets
Might as well go down as I am
And join the party

Yesterday

Yesterday was a desert all over again.
I left my footprints on her unblemished
Curves, both the black parts,
And the nearly white.
I did not feel thirsty for a second.
It was hot, but not unbearable.
When I felt like kissing the ground,
That is exactly what I did.
I made strange faces, sang songs
I heard my mother sing during
The childhood I never had, and if
I got really excited, I screamed
A bottomless scream that was without
Angst or malice. I could not remember
Whether it was dark or light the moment
I finally went to sleep, but here we are,
And hello, sunshine.

Poem for Venice

In one hour I will be at the station,
On my way to the future.
The past massages my temples
In this quiet lake of a hotel room
And my thoughts become a pebble
Rolling whichever way the Great Shoe
Kicks it along an alley growing
Ever more narrow by the second.
Some people have it better because
They get to stay. And one of them,
I imagine, is a woman in a white dress
Hanging her laundry and singing
As if she need not be heard
In this lifetime, and then a red
Balloon may come from out of the water
And arrive at her feet. She will take
The balloon and tie it around
Her door, so that the next child
Who passes by can untie the balloon
And carry its string in their fist, tightly,
Running off into the evening—

Ned

I drove ten thousand miles to visit
A friend, and when I reached
His doorstep, a gaunt, foreboding
Old man wearing a hat
That leered at me was standing there.
"Where's Ned?" I asked.
"Oh you must not have heard.
Ned and his two girls are far, far
Away." He made the gesture
Of three flying blackbirds,
And his hat seemed to be providing
The sound of wayward flight.
"The weeds live here now. And
Some fallen trees, the bees,
And perhaps the occasional
Stray dog or vagabond."
I scanned the place in front of me,
The house with its taped-up
Windows, depraved, ruined mouth
Of a door, dead branches
Frozen at the moment where
They must have been lunging
Towards the open kitchen window
When there was clearly no longer
Any kitchen by the time they arrived
On the lawn. I bowed my head
And fought back tears. I looked
Up again at the man. "You know,"
I began, "the summer we both
Got back after our first year

Of college, Ned couldn't wait to tell me
About his new invention. He said
That he found a way to please
A woman like no other with just
A styrofoam cup, a brown paper bag
And two nickels. The trick went
Like this. . ." Before I could go on,
I burst into a hysterical laughter,
And immediately even the man
Of sinister appearance joined in.
Soon we were both on the ground,
Grabbing at each other
For something hard to hold on to,
Just trying to keep our insides
Intact. The tears finally came out.

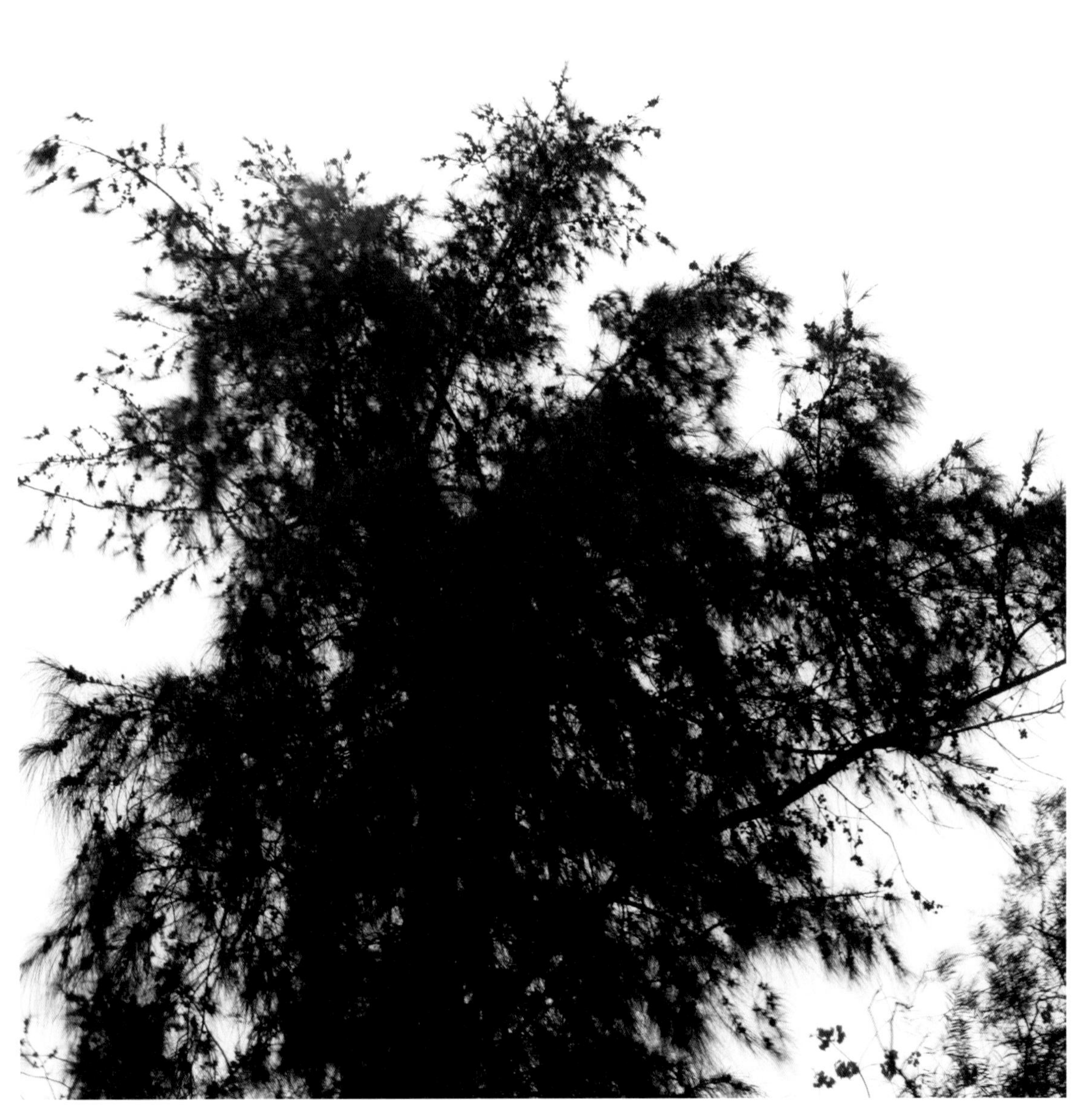

Politics of the Flesh

What is the smallest and yet most
Endless country in the world?
Your body, all five feet and six inches
And one hundred and ten pounds
Of it. Does this country ever go
To war? Every night, my dear.
Who is the President of this nation?
There is no President; he's dead,
But I will be the First Lady. Describe
To me the palace in which
You reside, First Lady.
The house is a grand shade of white
With onyx floors and high crimson
Ceilings, each room asking its walls
A question containing no answer.
To any stranger passing by
We are a universe perpetually in flames.

True Romance

The rainbow had been taunting us
With its beauty for the past half-hour.
We get it: you're precious
And fleeting, you with your delicate
Curves we can't touch or drink from
Or make love to with bittersweet
Strokes while thinking only thoughts
Of you, nothing else. The dirt
I am sitting on is wet with self-pity.
Brown, don't feel so bad. Honestly,
I'd rather be here, not up there,
And spend the rest of this afternoon
And the evening too
With your creature comforts
Beneath my naked body.

The Year of the Rat

A red truck is driving by,
Loud and insufferable
Just as a rat darts past
In the opposite direction.
I was born in the year of the Rat,
According to the Chinese Zodiac.
I am seated on a park bench
And see and hear both the truck
And the rat making their ways
Through the space that surrounds me,
But I feel no bigger or smaller
Than either of them. All things move
Towards the same finish line:
The rat, the truck, its driver,
The bench, the park, the half-eaten
Ham sandwich on top of the book
Next to me, the man who wrote
That book, words, poetry, civilization.
But no matter; for now the sun
Is in my lap, and it feels good.

Growing Up

You have to learn to do the dishes properly
Before you are able to go out on your own
Without telling us where you'll be.

You have to button your top button and play
The piano, and not until the clock hits nine
Can you go back to your room.

You have to do fifty push ups and a hundred
Jumping jacks. Jack and Jill went up the hill
Only once Jack was strong enough to carry her.

You have to know what's right or wrong
In this world. I felt your gym shorts before
I washed them. That shit will make you blind.

You have to give me your left hand as well.
You have to learn that there is nothing
More important in life than balance.

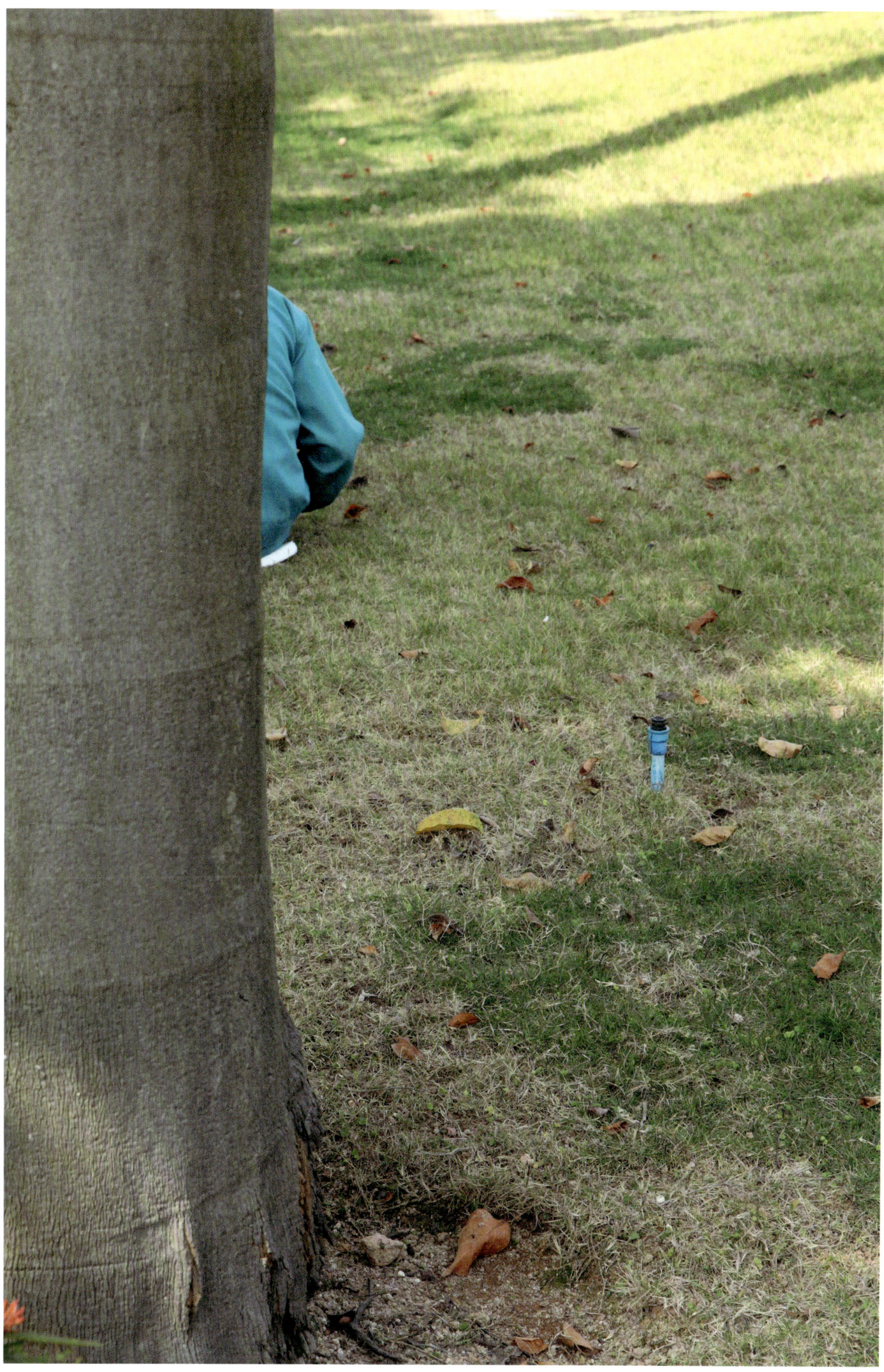

Fat

For Raymond Carver and Marlon Brando
Let me tell you about those early days,
Kid, when up was the only way, before
The fridge had to be locked up and my
Neighbor called to tell me that I left
My briefs in his washing machine.
It all seems so silly now, imagine
Me in the corner of a jukebox joint,
Brooding over that day's failures:
She kept looking at my wrists,
The back of my hands, finally
Refusing to hold it in any longer
And said to me, "I'm sorry,
But you're too thin and lonely
To make it in this town!" That
Was when l started eating. You could
Find me holding court in the burger shack,
Over my two hamburgers, French fries,
A slice of apple pie a la mode, and
When the waitress looked at me,
Not without a hint of concern,
I smiled my vanilla smile and told her,
"Oh, just think, the things we'll do
And the places
we'll go!"

2014

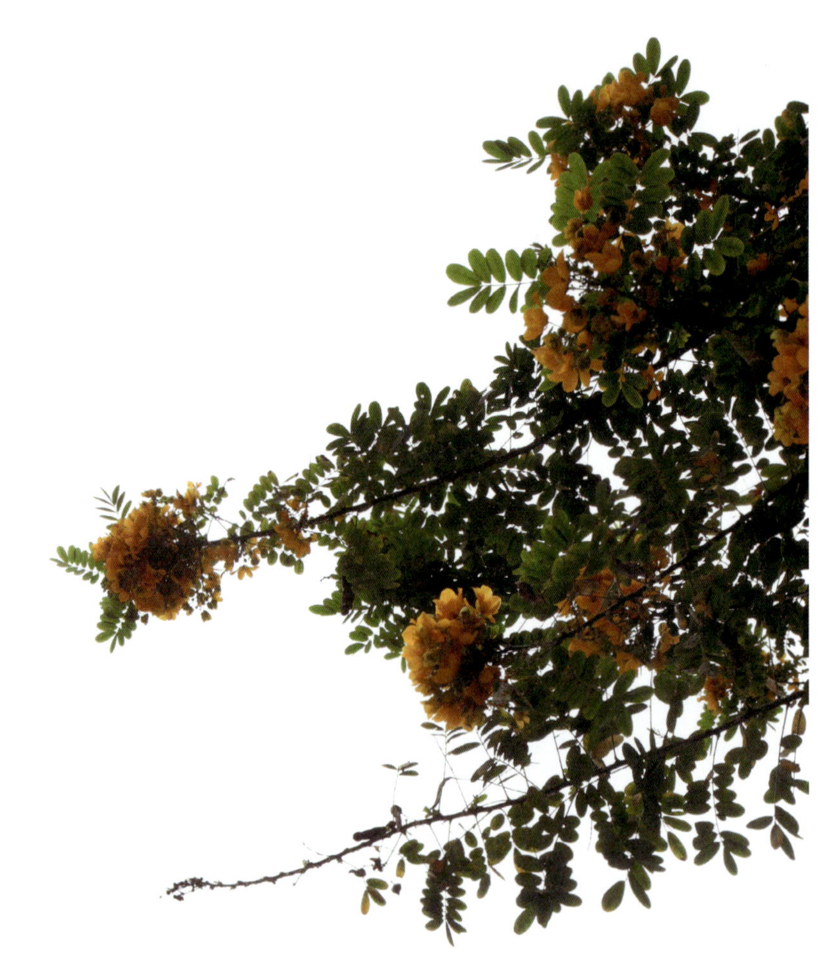

Untitled

Hand over eyes
Glove over hand
Black over glove
Nothing over black
Except your voice
On the other end
Of a tunnel that begins
At the sun's last breath

The Music

I am in the middle of nowhere, an open field,
Searching for my inner child in a blade
Of grass, and then I hear it: the music,
Which sounds like unnameable colors
Coming from a direction I cannot fathom.
I look all around and see nothing
But the even landscape, the sun, no clouds.
The music is getting louder. It reminds me
Of Japan, though I have never been there.
I dance nervously, as if I am being watched
And I am not supposed to remain still.
There is a hole in the seat of my pants.
I feel my face getting hot. Am I the only one
That hears it? Of course I am,
There's nobody here. The music
Getting faster now, the melody
More confrontational. The ground
Is so green, so glorious and virginal,
And this music clearly has no regard
For beauty, its attack more vicious
With every note, I fear for my safety.
I stop dancing and start running for my life.

I don't know where I must run to, I am
Just running out of an instinct for survival.
As far as the eye can see, this place
Looks the same all over and goes on forever.
It is alive with the sound of music.

Wanted

You are an unassuming silhouette
On a beige wall. You carried grief
For the future while you were inside
Your mother. You were not born
With the ability to make strangers,
Especially of the opposite sex, feel safe
In your presence. You implode upon
Getting into a handshake with someone
Whose palms know no sweat.
You do not believe in an afterlife.
You believe in an afterlife.
You cringe at the sight of a telephone
But high places make you feel fantastic
And the first five seconds of standing
On a casino floor even more so.
But you do not even have enough change
On you for a single chip. You have what
It takes to sharpen a pencil. You can,
On a good day, press the right buttons
So that the sky becomes your baseball cap
And magic happens in between each blink.

2015

Four People

1.

I look up at the sky and see more beauty
Jumping out of the windows of clouds
Than I could hope to catch
As my younger self.

2.

Two lonely roads are touching heads
In a desolate forest. A mile
To the east, a voluptuous stream.
And sitting in a tree, the man dressed
As a bat was wondering where on earth
He could find the best silence.

3.

Late in life the magician acquired a dream
That visits him several times a year:
He is eating at a Chinese restaurant
In a nameless American city somewhere
In the Midwest, and at the end of the meal
He cracks open his fortune cookie
And every time it says the same thing:
"Has your work come to nothing?
No, it has come to this."

Purpose

To kiss a doorbell. To daydream naked
Into the yellow pages. To whisper
Sweet nothings over a graveyard
Full of strangers. To stare at the sun
Until it becomes a black dot.
To visit Oblivion. To visit Tahiti.
To walk into a movie theater
Wearing nothing but the news.
To replace the cookie jar
On the top shelf with a bronze Buddha.
To stop asking the sea for closure.
To write love letters at night
While trying not to think of
A purple elephant. To hold indeterminacy
Hostage, permanently. To pick a number
From one to a million, and to build
A life around that number.
To write a blank cheque
Addressed to the rain.
To tip generously with wishes.
To get the face you deserve.
To watch the sunset
With your eyes closed.
To get out of here
With Sinatra singing ever so softly
In the background

Vincent

The waves of the sky are washing
The day off my boots. I study
My reflection in a tree, which sings
Back to me in a playful tone
The outline of a skull. All around
The shirts of children are laughing
And chasing each other's tails.
I smile. I ask a flower for her name
And she whispers ever so timidly,
"Blue." I follow a stranger's shadow
Through a long alleyway, and watch
With sorrow and longing as it goes
From red to green, to brown, to violet.
I look up at the sky and squint. The moon
Is the color of remembering.

June

I am that which is idle on a summer day.
I am the mouth that does not move.
I am the dish that parts the beef like a sea.
I am the wind's last legs at dusk.
I am six feet short of the moon,
Watching you as you sleep, and you,
Who came to my breath, perhaps expecting me
To turn up around the corner in the rain,
Like a memory of Paris, so I close my eyes
And kiss you as if I was there.

The Shape of Silence

Drifting down the river
Of another pink morning
I think about how the empty page
Emits its own particular light,
And were a shadow to fall upon it
That, too, is but another kind of writing.
Imagine reading a novel
Where instead of looking at the words
Your gaze was fixed on the spaces
Between them. When you get to the end,
What would you say of what you saw and felt?
I close the book and look up.
A thin blue line is falling asleep on the horizon
As the breeze reaches the end of its lullaby.
I study what's left of my reflection in the water.
I see now that your nakedness was never mine.

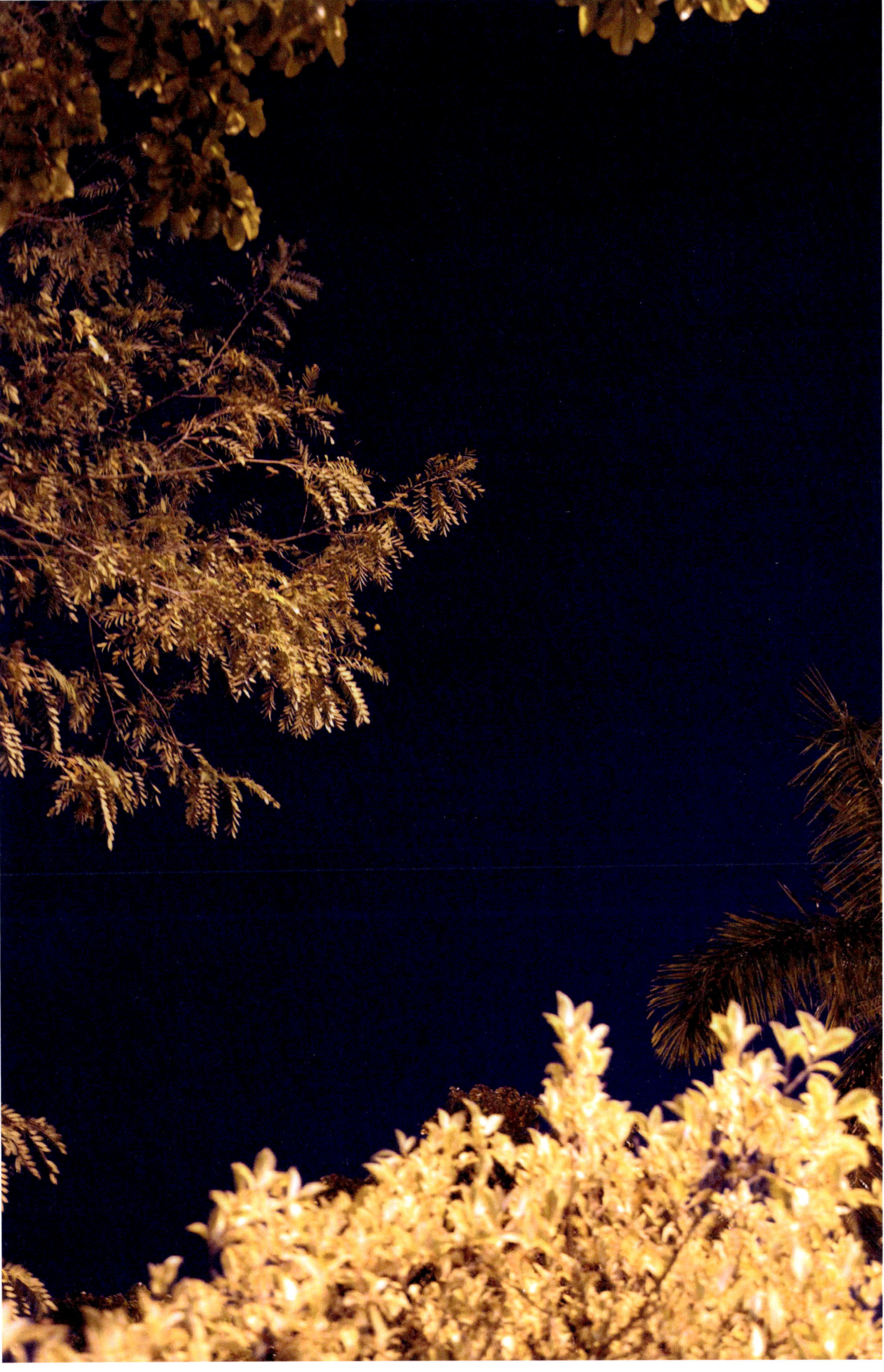

2016

Nostalgia

Here is where I have come
To rest my head, this blue
Dormitory in which I once took
A shower while staring at
A pointless bathtub filled
With the unspeakable. I open
The curtains that kept me hidden
On many solitary nights, and look
At the red brick house across, where
I met a girl named Beth
My first week here, Beth
Who would forget me later.
I walk down the green hallway and,
Passing the door marked '210',
Remember a clear canister of yellow
Fluid placed at the foot one Sunday
Morning, perhaps a bad omen or
Perhaps signifying nothing at all.
I caress the mouth of the water fountain,
Which I only drank from once or twice,
Avoiding it as I found the taste of water,
As I do now, too neutral.
Coming to an open door, I pause;
They were sitting inconspicuously,
Music dim in the background,
Yet I raced through scenarios
Of unlikely betrayal that were needed
For nourishment, for edge. She asked
Me what was wrong, and I kept walking.
I see a cigarette butt on the ground

And think of the giant who once told me
Through drained eyes that they made him
Throw up. I reach the end of the floor,
Noticing the rug has not been changed,
Nor the odor that keeps an anxious
Sensation of the past always biting
On the heels of now, of the presence
Of people known and then unknown,
Of a dull afterglow that hovers
As I call winter by its name.

Undated

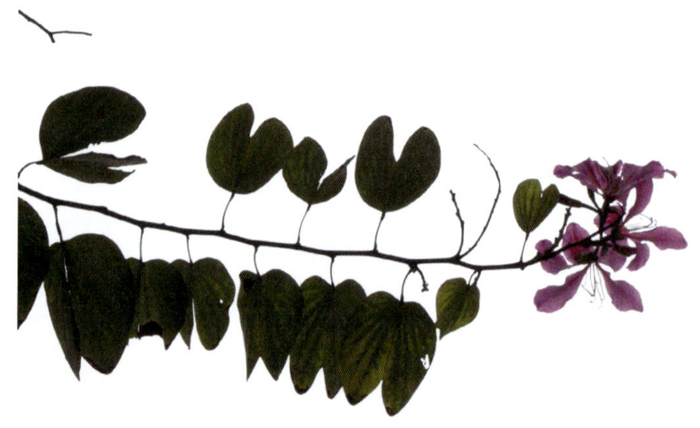

Mass Appeal

For John Wall Barger

You could tell by the smell of their attention spans
That the crowd was getting restless, like a retirement home.
Fair enough.
It isn't every day a comedian gets on stage
With a whale and last month's Playboy for props.
Not to mention the fact that the jokes being rattled
Out of their cage in early-evening single file
Weren't jokes at all, really. More like the Fat Lady
In a recording booth, chain-smoking and refusing
To hand out a single note. It was a scene
Of pitch-perfect dissolution, enough to send the clowns
Who were washing dishes in the ladies' room
Back on rural turf, as they heard through the grapevine
That the vegetables had finally matured. But where
Did he go wrong? All he wanted was to re-enact
A situation he once read about, where a psychopathic
Thespian built a gated garden and threw away
The key. That sounds like a plan to me, don't you think?

Drawing

She draws a flower with her blood,
The petals a crisscross of crimson
On the ink trodden page. It was
The last resort after a long day
Of trying and failing. She lets
The blood flow freely as
Red dries into haphazard blots
Of shades of black and grey.
There was a point
At which it could have been
Considered finished,
But she reminded herself
Of an earlier lesson—to never trust
The first sign of satisfaction.

Rage

The sun is out today, and I
Am at my desk, on the typewriter.
The windows are slightly open
And a wisp of wind passes,
Ruffling the translucent curtains
Like a sigh. The sun is out
And I type away, all those things
That speak to me on an afternoon
When the rage is running
Through my veins, the throb
In my temple a shade of bruised meat;
A bloom of red flora rushes forth.

The Painter

And after the party the guests
Shuffled out in single file. He watched
By the corridor, like the sky, perhaps,
Although to actually say farewell
Would be to intrude on his necessary
Brooding. Once the door closed, the drinks
Would begin, him, an easel nursing
An unfinished commission to be doted on,
But not without a trace of disdain combined
With masturbatory self-pity; certain
Women of society had that effect on him.
A flush of light on the facial region seemed
Especially difficult this evening, as she
Had said something earlier, unexpected,
And the aura of mystique was ruined. Morning
Approached without much progress. He picked
Up a can of white paint mixed with medium
And splashed the surface, letting the stuff
Run its course. Standing in front
Of the picture, hands on hips,
He declared the painting finished.

Again

My shoelaces bruise with the wine of sorrow.
Time after time I have hurled paint
Against this white wall, waiting for my mother,
Or a girlfriend to come out of the mess,
As if such things hide in pigment, but the act
Itself betrays my selfish whimsy, and there
Is no one to blame but the maid,
She who wipes and scrubs out of love,
Out of wanting to grant me the freedom
A world like ours does not forgive;
She speaks in two- or three-word phrases,
But in her eyes rests a valley of knowing
Empathy, a landscape that says,
"It is not too much to ask. Your solitude
Is like the disappearance of stars. I had
A son like you once, and through you,
I can get it right this time." I stand before
What I have done and coax myself
Into believing all that could be true,
And the meaning that does not reveal
Its body under so much stubborn,
Seductive cloth is what we chase
In order to find the I in the midst
Of a house of mirrors set on fire as the days
Undo themselves yet again, and again.

It

They call it many things, but my favorite
Word for it has to be "juice." I haven't slept
In five days and four nights, but now
I'm driving down to Mexico City,
Where the action is, where the bodies are,
And it becomes impossible
To think about anything else. I pass
Strange, truly strange rocks along the highway,
Monsters that make my skin crawl, almost
Enough for me to hurl the last three rolls
Of expired film I have left at them. The road
Starts caving in the further I go
Into crepuscular redness; my stomach turns
At the sight of what may or may not
Be a child lying face down in a black pool.
The wind strokes my hair, as if assuring that this
Is the price to pay for unknown pleasures.

A Situation

He didn't like the sight of handcuffs
On thin wrists, but there was no other
Option, it seemed, so handcuffs it was.
"Can you get me a glass of water
Or something?" Never one
For small talk, he refused to answer,
Paced nervously while waiting
For further instructions. It wasn't that
He emerged from dire beginnings, or
Was ever neglected by his family,
There just wasn't much else
He could do in life, or wanted to, especially
Now that he was this deep in the game.
"Let's work something out. How much
Are they paying you if this goes down?
Help me get out of here and we'll go
To the nearest bank, and I'll give you
A million dollars, how about that?"
What was the point? A million dollars
To him was no better than
A jail cell in Bermuda with a view
Of the beach. He wasn't in it for the cash.
"What we have here is. . .failure
To communicate." He paused,
The corners of his mouth launching
Into the start of a smile. He knew
That line from somewhere. Where
Was it? Oh yeah, the good ol' days.

"A"

Who is this stranger, this man
Who looks as if he just arrived
From wilder shores of mirth,
An uneaten peach in his mouth, a
Screwdriver peeking out of one sock,
His eyes never quite looking
At anything, perhaps because
They have already seen all
There is to see in a lifetime,
And know that the only tale
That can be told from such sights
Is an interminable silence?

Prelude

It started out like
Any other night. He
Was a study
In concentrated alienation,
Occupying a solitude somewhere
Between brutal nerve
And immaculate sensibility.
A gambling man, he was less
About the chips
Or even the cards, wanting
Merely to walk in and breathe
The tense air, his dread
Crossing the tightrope
Of masochistic anticipation.
When he got dressed, it was
With diffident care, making sure
To look proper but inconspicuous.
Unpredictable scenarios
Were planned in advance, as if
One could fashion chance
Out of thin air.

As for her, she was nobody
At this moment. She could
Be anybody in the house,
And he would know
When the time was right.

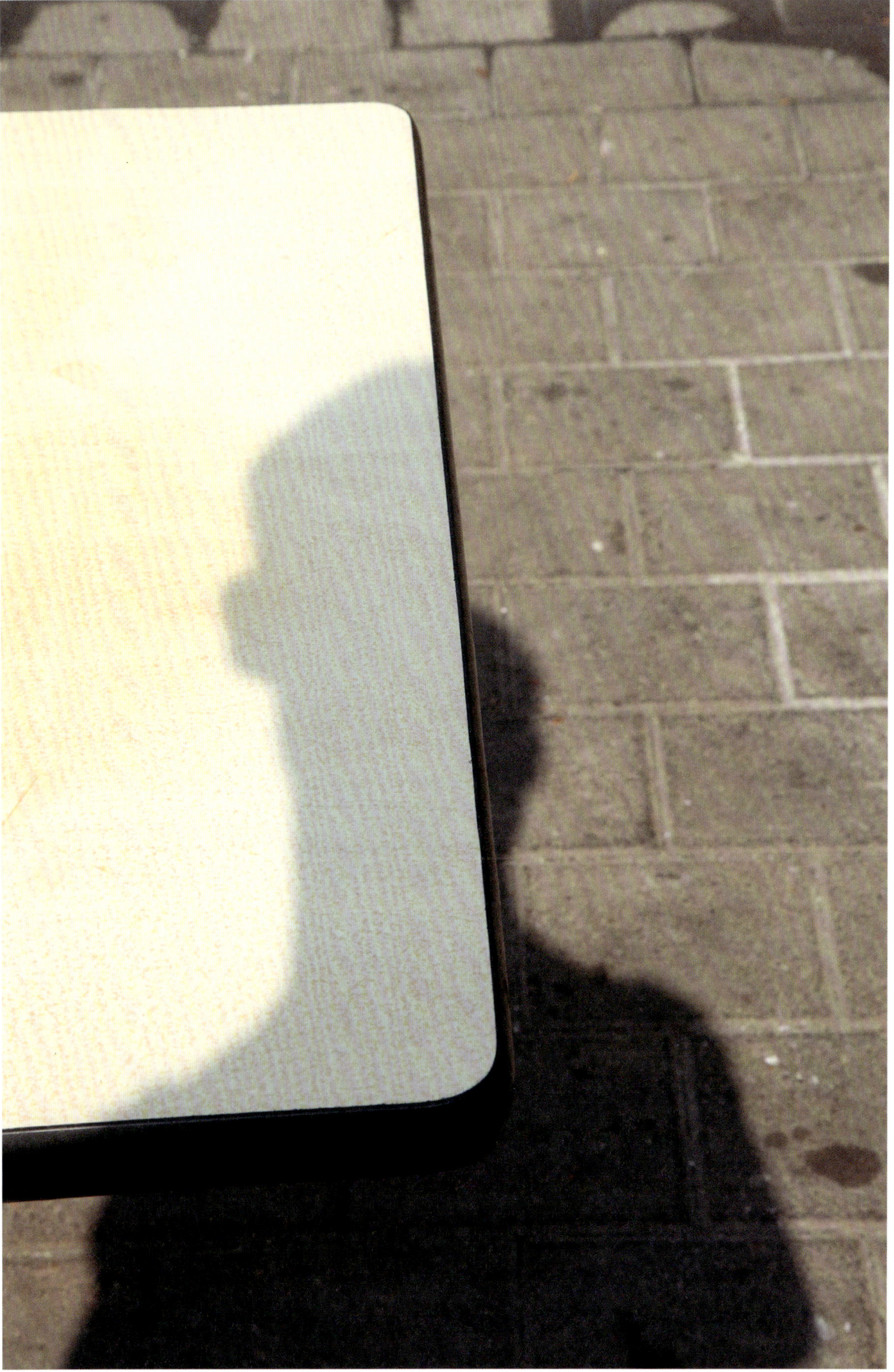

All photography by Matthew Wong

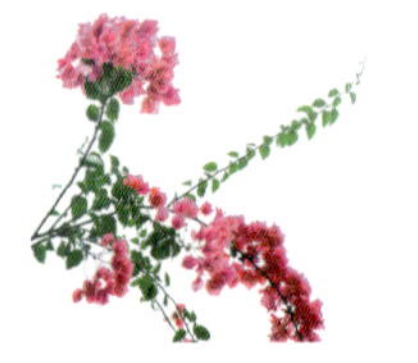

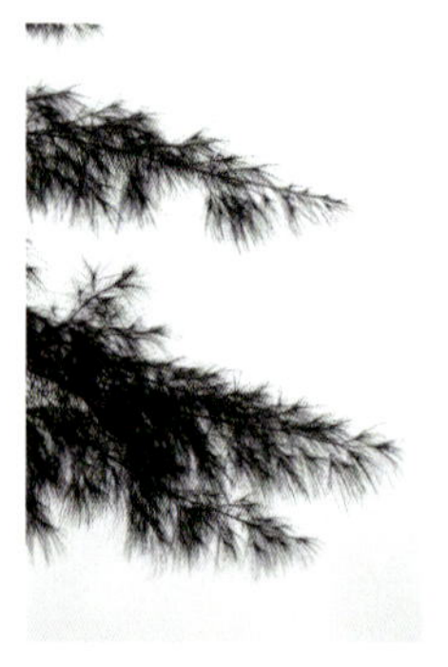

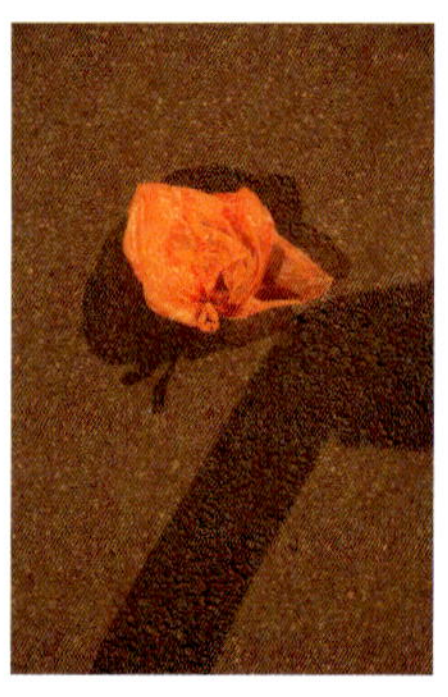

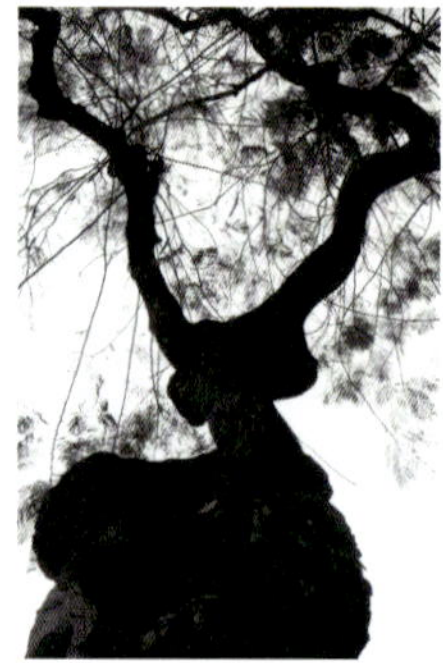

UNTITLED (3/23/2013)
2013, digital photography

UNTITLED (2/17/2013)
2013, digital photography

UNTITLED (8/25/2008)
2008, digital photography

UNTITLED (2/15/2013)
2013, digital photography

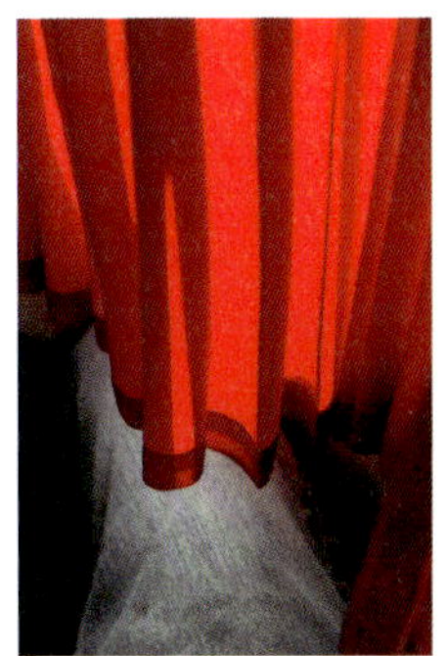

UNTITLED (8/15/2008)
2008, digital photography

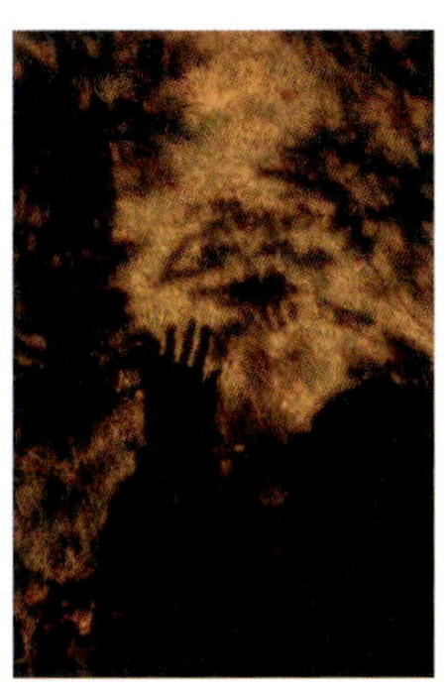

UNTITLED (7/29/2008)
2008, digital photography

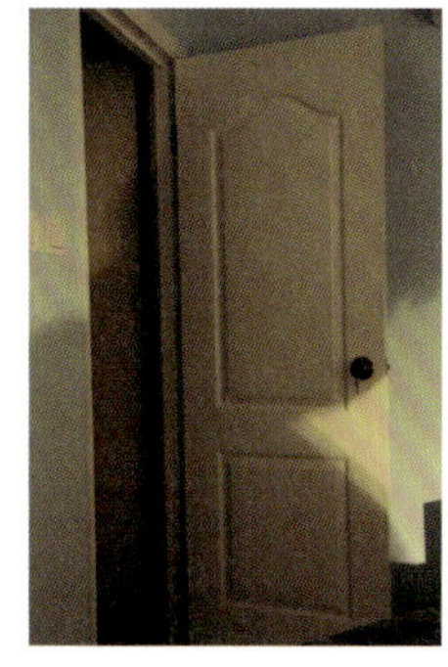

UNTITLED (1/3/2008)
2008, digital photography

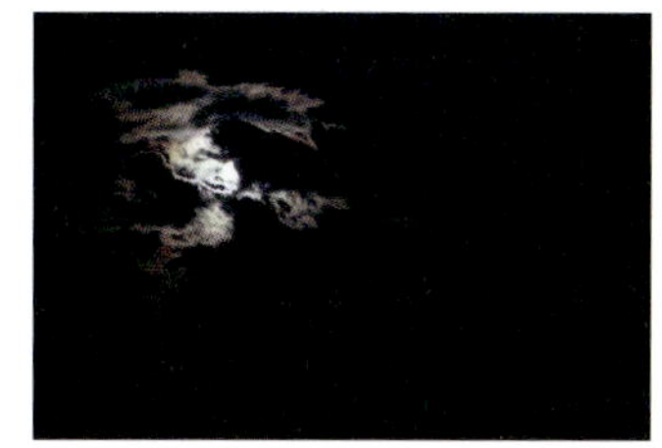

UNTITLED (3/6/2010)
2010, digital photography

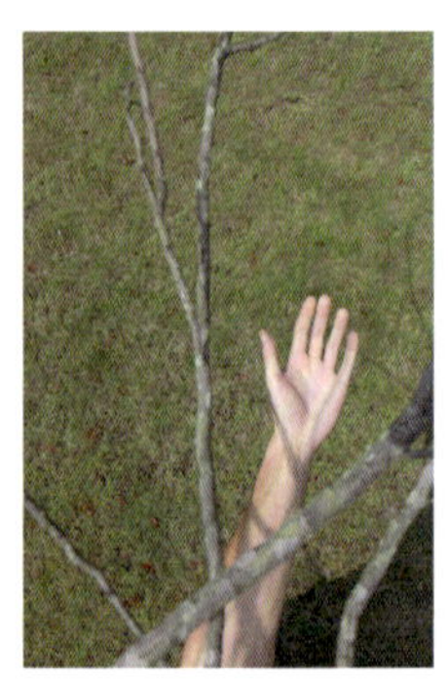

UNTITLED (5/12/2008)
2008, digital photography

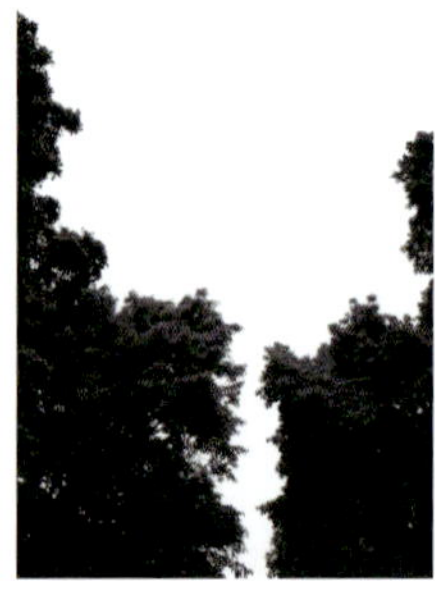

UNTITLED (1/16/2008)
2008, digital photography

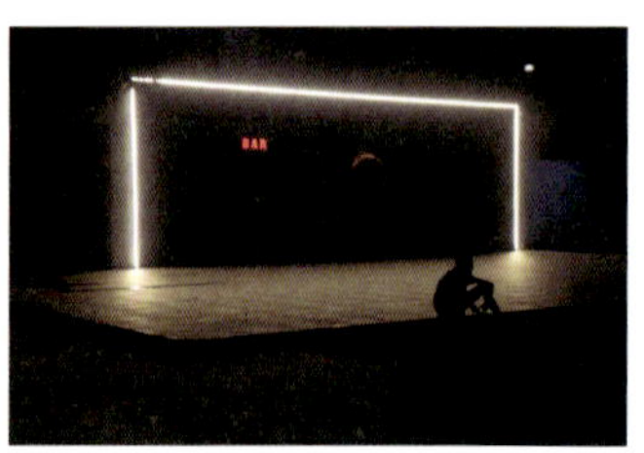

UNTITLED (3/25/2009)
2009, digital photography

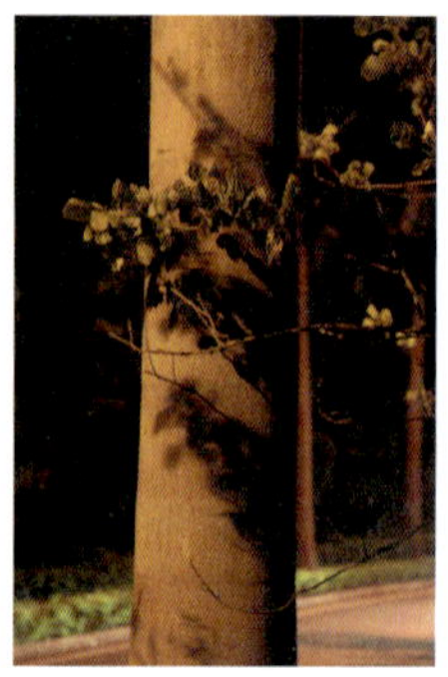

UNTITLED (12/28/2008)
2008, digital photography

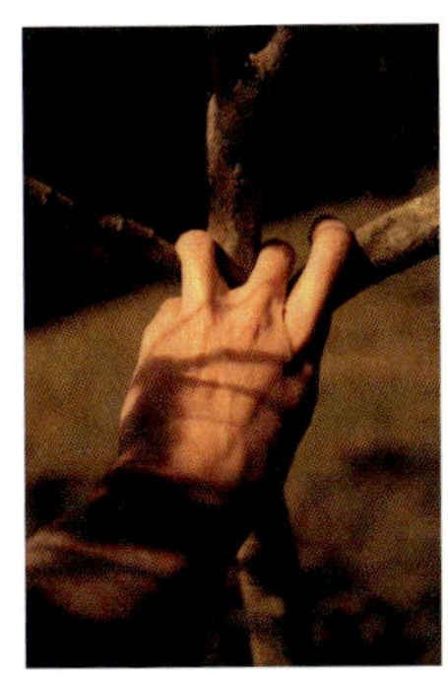

UNTITLED (7/26/2008)
2008, digital photography

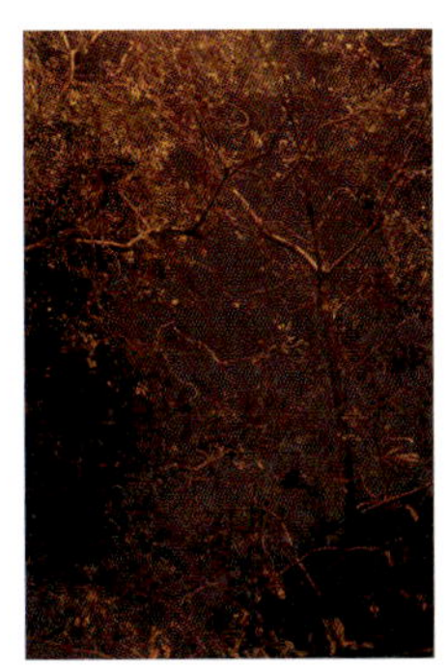

UNTITLED (4/8/2013)
2013, digital photography

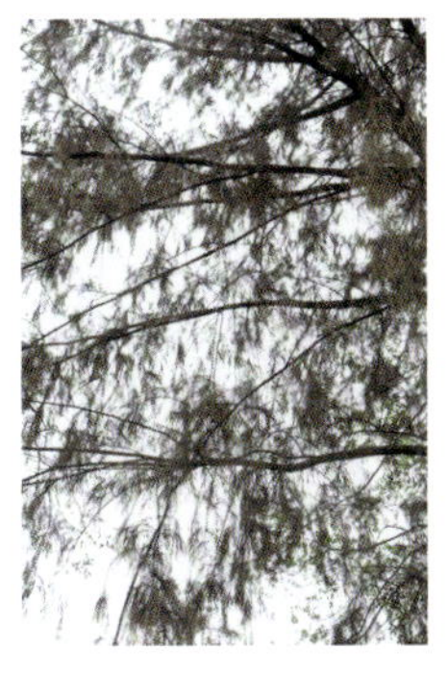

UNTITLED (4/8/2013)
2013, digital photography

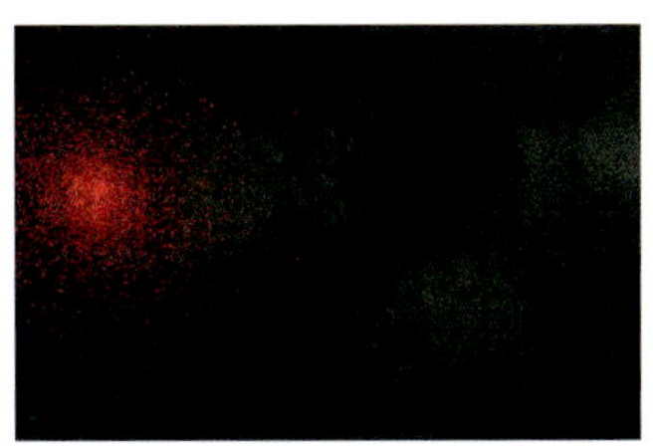

UNTITLED (4/2/2013)
2013, digital photography

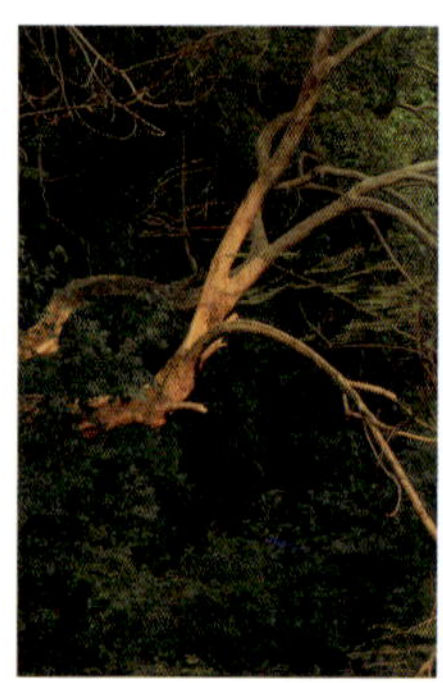

UNTITLED (3/23/2013)
2013, digital photography

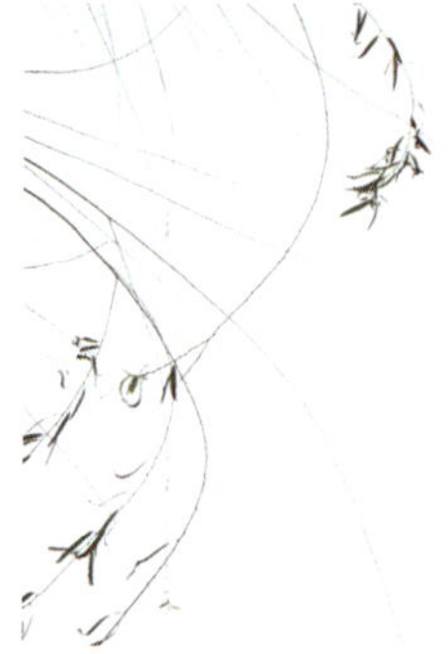

UNTITLED (3/27/2013)
2013, digital photography

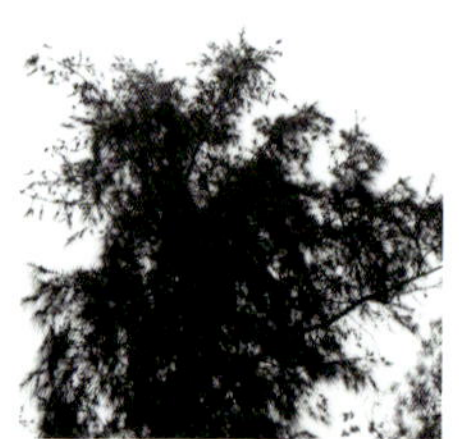

UNTITLED (3/25/2013)
2013, digital photography

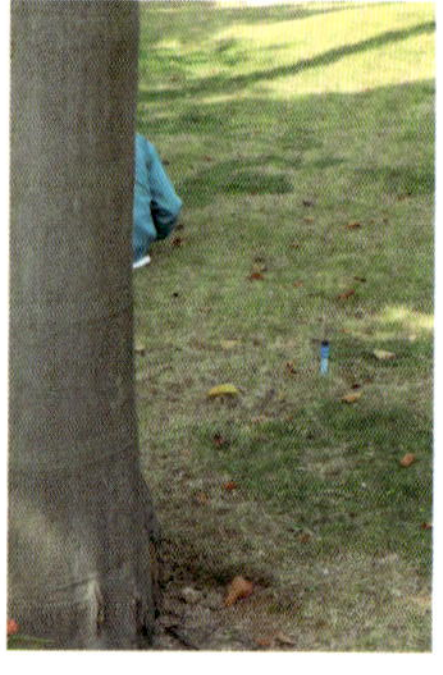

UNTITLED (9/18/2008)
2008, digital photography

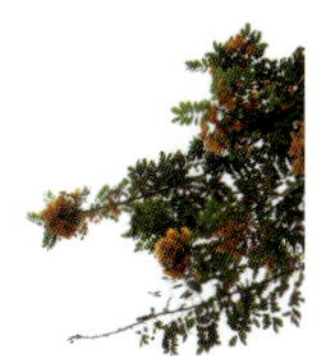

UNTITLED (2/26/2013)
2013, digital photography

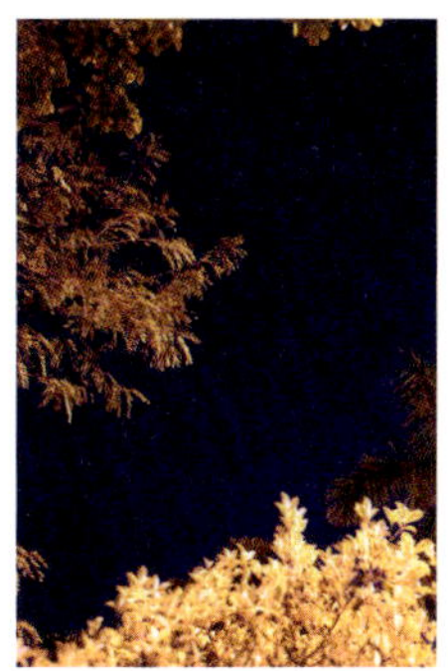

UNTITLED (9/18/2008)
2008, digital photography

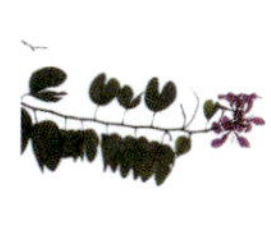

UNTITLED (2/24/2013)
2013, digital photography

UNTITLED (9/18/2008)
2008, digital photography

Printed in an edition of 2,000

Poems and photographs
© 2024, 2025 The Matthew Wong Foundation
MatthewWongFoundation.com
Introduction © John Yau
Essay © John Wall Barger
Edited and designed by John Cheim
ISBN 979-8-218-52976-5
Printed in Italy by Graphicom